Internet
in an Hour
for Seniors

Jennifer Frew
Don Mayo
Kathy Berkemeyer

Acknowledgements

To Monique "scissorhands" Peterson for doing that voodoo that you do so well.

Jennifer Frew

To Jen: May we live so long!

Don Mayo

Dedicated to the memory of my parents, John and Gert Madden.

Kathy Berkemeyer

Managing Editor	Technical Editors	English Editor	Illustrations	Design and Layout
Jennifer Frew	Monique Peterson Cathy Vesecky	Monique Peterson	Ryan Sather	Maria Kardasheva Midori Nakamura Shu Chen Paul Wray

Contents

Introduction.. iv

Basics

Netscape
Netscape Navigator: 1 2
Netscape Navigator: 2 7
Netscape Navigator: 3 10
Netscape Messenger: 4 14
Netscape Messenger: 5 23
Netscape Messenger: 6 33

Internet Explorer
Microsoft Internet Explorer: 7 38
Microsoft Internet Explorer: 8 43
Microsoft Internet Explorer: 9 46
Outlook Express: 10 50
Outlook Express: 11 62
Outlook Express: 12 71

America Online
America Online: 13 77
America Online: 14 81
America Online: 15 85
America Online E-mail: 16 90
America Online E-mail: 17 95
America Online E-mail: 18 100

Search Engines
Search Engines: 19 105
Search Engines: 20 108
Search Engines: 21 112

Web Resources

Leisure-Time Pleasures
What's Cooking? 118
Gourmet Goodies Online............................... 124
How Does Your Garden Grow?........................ 127
Fun and Games... 131
Arts & Crafts 137

Travel Sites
Cheap Seats (Airfare)............................... 141
Travel Adventures 145

All in the Family
Family Trees.. 150
Grandparenting... 155
Net Pet Care.. 158

Just for Seniors
Resources Galore...................................... 162
Advocacy and Legislation........................... 169
Home Is Where the Heart Is 173
Medical Advice 179

Money Matters
Watching Your Money Grow............................ 187

Read All About It
Extra! Extra! Read All About It!.................... 192
Online Magazines....................................... 196
Newsgroups 201
Mailing Lists... 207

Computer Troubleshooting
Computer Savvy Seniors.............................. 212
URL Troubleshooting: Addressee Unknown........... 215

Support
Support Resources.................................... 219

Contents

Appendices

Appendix A: Emoticons and Abbreviations.............221
Appendix B: Netiquette..............................223
Appendix C: Timesaving Tools 225
Glossary 228

Index 239

Introduction

This Book is Designed for You . . .

if you are new to the Internet or you are not sure what kind of information is available to you online.

The Internet is a vast and ever-growing resource where you can find information and entertainment. This book shows you where and how to find the best resources available.

This book has two main sections, Internet Basics and Web Resources.

Internet Basics

In Internet Basics, you can learn how to:

- Use Netscape Navigator 4 to browse the World Wide Web.
- Send and receive e-mail messages with Netscape Messenger.
- Use Internet Explorer 4 to browse the World Wide Web.
- Send and receive e-mail messages with Microsoft Outlook Express.
- Access the Internet using America Online 4.
- Send and receive e-mail messages with America Online.
- Find information on the Web with search engines.

Web Resources

Web Resources shows you ways you can use the Web to find both practical and fun information.

Web Resources is organized by general categories (such as Leisure-Time Pleasures, Monetary Matters, Just for Seniors), then by topics (such as What's Cooking?, Watching Your Money Grow, and Online Magazines).

Each topic showcases top Web sites that offer excellent information. The Web site listings provide you with the site's URL (Web address) and a brief description of how the site can help you. In many cases an illustration of the Web site is also provided.

What Do I Need to Use This Book?

This book assumes that you have some general knowledge and experience with computers, and that you already know how to perform the following tasks:

- Use a mouse (double-click, etc.).
- Make your way around Microsoft Windows 95.
- Install and run programs.

If you are completely new to computers as well as the Internet, you may want to refer to DDC's **Learning Microsoft Windows 95** or **Learning the Internet**.

This book also assumes that you have access to browser applications such as Microsoft Internet Explorer 4.0, Netscape Navigator 4.0, or America Online 4.

✔ *If you do not currently have these applications, contact your Internet Service Provider for instructions on how to download them. You can also use other browsers or previous versions such as Explorer 3.0, Navigator 3.0, or AOL 3.0 to browse the Web.*

You must have an Internet connection. How to get connected to the Internet is not covered in this book.

Please read over the following list of "must haves" to ensure that you are ready to be connected to the Internet.

- A computer (with a recommended minimum of 16 MB of RAM) and a modem port.

- A modem (with a recommended minimum speed of 14.4kbps, and suggested speed of 28.8kbps) that is connected to an analog phone line (assuming you are not using a direct Internet connection through your library, corporation, etc.).

- Established access to the Internet through an online service, independent Internet service provider, etc.

- A great deal of patience. The Internet is a fun and exciting place. But getting connected can be frustrating at times. Expect to run into occasional glitches, to get disconnected from time to time, and to experience occasional difficulty in viewing certain Web pages or features. The more up-to-date your equipment and software are, however, the less difficulty you will probably experience.

Internet Cautions

ACCURACY: Be cautious not to believe everything on the Internet. Almost anyone can publish information on the Internet, and since there is no Internet editor or monitor, some information may be false. All information found on the World Wide Web should be checked for accuracy through additional reputable sources.

SECURITY: When sending information over the Internet, be prepared to let the world have access to it. Computer hackers can find ways to access anything that you send to anyone over the Internet, including e-mail. Be cautious when sending confidential information to anyone.

VIRUSES: These small, usually destructive computer programs hide inside of innocent-looking programs. Once a virus is executed, it attaches itself to other programs. When triggered, often by the occurrence of a date or time on the computer's internal clock/calendar, it executes a nuisance or damaging function, such as displaying a message on your screen, corrupting your files, or reformatting your hard disk.

- Netscape Navigator: 1
- Netscape Navigator: 2
- Netscape Navigator: 3
- Netscape Messenger: 4
- Netscape Messenger: 5
- Netscape Messenger: 6
- Microsoft Internet Explorer: 7
- Microsoft Internet Explorer: 8
- Microsoft Internet Explorer: 9
- Outlook Express: 10
- Outlook Express: 11
- Outlook Express: 12
- America Online: 13
- America Online: 14
- America Online: 15
- America Online E-mail: 16
- America Online E-mail: 17
- America Online E-mail: 18
- Search Engines: 19
- Search Engines: 20
- Search Engines: 21

BASICS

Netscape Navigator: 1

◆ About Netscape Navigator
◆ Start Netscape Navigator
◆ Increase Font Size ◆ The Netscape Screen
◆ Exit Netscape Navigator

About Netscape Navigator

- This chapter focuses on Netscape Navigator 4.0, the Internet browser component of Netscape Communicator. Netscape Messenger, the e-mail component, is covered in Chapters 4-6.

Start Netscape Navigator

1. Click the Start button [Start].

2. Click Programs, Netscape Communicator, Netscape Navigator.

   OR

   If you have a shortcut to Netscape Communicator

   on your desktop, double-click it to start Netscape Navigator.

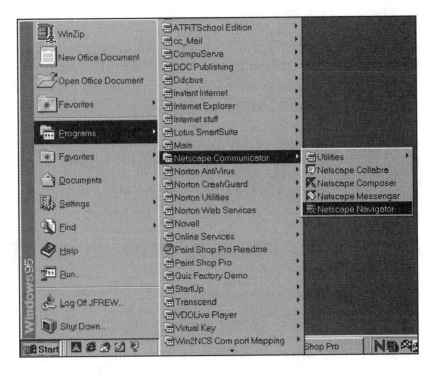

✔ *The first time you start Netscape Communicator, the New Profile Setup dialog box appears. Enter e-mail and service provider information in the dialog boxes that appear. If you do not know the information, you can leave it blank until you are ready to fill it in. See the sections on Netscape Messenger in this book for more information.*

Increase Font Size

■ For larger on screen text, Netscape allows you to increase font size. All Web sites that you view will use the larger font.

To increase font size:

1. Click View.

2. Click Increase Font.

   ✔ *You can repeat the above steps until you find a size that you like.*

The Netscape Screen

- The Netscape Navigator screen contains features that help you explore the Internet. Some of these features are constant and some change depending on the task attempted or completed.

Title bar

Displays the name of the program (Netscape) and the current Web page (Welcome to Netscape).

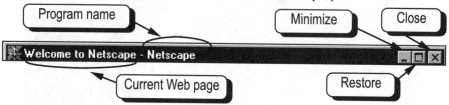

Menu bar

Displays drop-down lists of Netscape commands.

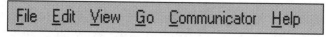

Navigation toolbar

Contains buttons for online activity. The name and icon on each button identify the command.

✔ *If the toolbar buttons are not visible, open the View menu and click Show Navigation Toolbar.*

Location toolbar

The electronic address of the current Web page displays in the Location field. You can also type the Web page address, called a Uniform Resource Locator (URL), in the Location field and press Enter to access it.

✔ *If the Location toolbar is not visible, open the View menu and click Show Location Toolbar.*

The Bookmarks QuickFile button is also on the Location toolbar. Click to view a list of sites that you have bookmarked for quick access. (For more on Bookmarks, see page 11.)

Personal toolbar

Contains buttons or links that you add to connect to your favorite sites. You can delete the default buttons (shown below) and add your own by displaying the desired Web site and dragging the Location icon onto the Personal toolbar.

Netscape's status indicator

Netscape's icon pulses when Netscape is processing a command. Click to return to Netscape's home page.

Status bar

When a Web page is opening, the Status bar indicates the downloading progress and the security level of the page being loaded. When you place the cursor over a hyperlink, the Status bar displays the URL of the link.

Component toolbar

The buttons on this toolbar link to other Netscape components: Navigator, Messenger Mailbox, Collabra Discussions, and Page Composer.

Exit Netscape Navigator

- Exiting Netscape Navigator and disconnecting from your Internet Service Provider (ISP) are two separate steps. You can disconnect from your service provider and still have Netscape Navigator open. You can also disconnect from Navigator and still have your ISP open.

- You may want to disconnect from your ISP and keep Netscape open to:

  - Read information obtained from the Web

  - Access information stored on your hard disk using Netscape

  - Compose e-mail to send later

- If you don't disconnect from your ISP and you pay an hourly rate, you will continue incurring charges.

  ✔ *You can disconnect from your ISP and still view Web information accessed during the current session by using the Back and Forward toolbar buttons. Your computer stores the visited sites in its memory.*

Netscape Navigator: 2

◆ The Navigation Toolbar
◆ Open World Wide Web Sites

The Navigation Toolbar

■ The Netscape Navigation toolbar displays buttons for Netscape's most commonly used commands. Note that each button contains an icon and a word describing the button's function. Choosing any of these buttons activates the indicated task immediately.

■ If the Navigation toolbar is not visible, select Show Navigation Toolbar from the View menu.

 Moves back through pages previously displayed. Back is available only if you have moved around among Web pages in the current Navigator session; otherwise, it is dimmed.

 Moves forward through pages previously displayed. Forward is available only if you have used the Back button; otherwise, it is dimmed.

 Reloads the currently displayed Web page. Use this button if the current page is taking too long to display or to update the current page with any changes that may have occurred since the page was downloaded.

 Displays the home page.

Displays Netscape's Net Search Page. You can select one of several search tools from this page.

 Displays a menu with helpful links to Internet sites that contain search tools and services.

 Prints the displayed page, topic, or article.

 Displays security information for the displayed Web page as well as information on Netscape security features.

 Stops the loading of a Web page.

Open World Wide Web Sites

- There are several ways to access a Web site. If you know the site's address, you can enter the correct Web address (URL) on the Location field on the Location toolbar.

- If the address you are entering is the address of a site you have visited recently or that you have bookmarked (see page 11 for more information on Bookmarks), you will notice as you begin to type the address that Netscape attempts to complete it for you. If the address that Netscape suggests is the one you want, press Enter.

- If the address that Netscape suggests is not correct, keep typing to complete the desired address and then press Enter. Or, you can click the down arrow next to the Location field to view a list of other possible matches, select an address, and press Enter.

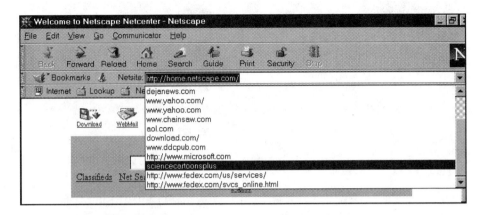

- There are a couple of shortcuts for entering URL addresses. One shortcut involves omitting the **http://www.** prefix from the Web address. Netscape assumes the **http://** protocol and the **www** that indicates that the site is located on the Web.

- If you are trying to connect to a company Web site, entering the company name is generally sufficient. Netscape assumes the **.com** suffix. For example, entering **ddcpublishing** on the location line and pressing Enter would reach the **http://www.ddcpub.com** address.

  ✔ *Don't be discouraged if you can't connect to the World Wide Web site immediately. The site may be offline temporarily. The site may also be very busy with other users trying to access it. Be sure the URL is typed accurately. Occasionally, it takes several tries to connect to a site.*

Netscape Navigator: 3

◆ History List ◆ Bookmarks
◆ Add Bookmarks ◆ Delete Bookmarks
◆ Print Web Pages

History List

- While you move back and forth among Web sites, Netscape automatically records each of these site locations in a History list, which is temporarily stored on your computer.

- You can use the History list to track or view sites that you have recently visited. The History list is an easy way to see the path you followed to get to a particular Web page.

- To view the History list, click History on the Communicator menu, or press Ctrl+H. To link to a site shown in the History list, double-click on it.

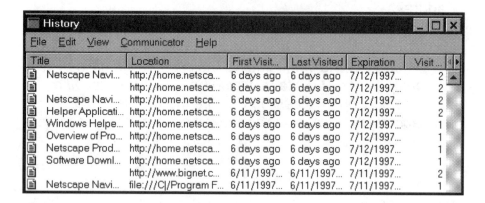

Bookmarks

- A Bookmark is a placeholder containing the title and URL of a Web page that, when selected, links directly to that page. If you find a Web site that you like and want to revisit, you can create a Bookmark to record its location. (See **Add Bookmarks** below.)

- The Netscape Bookmark feature maintains permanent records of the Web sites in your Bookmark files so that you can return to them easily.

- You can view the Bookmarks menu by selecting Bookmarks from the Communicator menu or by clicking on the Bookmarks QuickFile button  on the Location toolbar. The drop-down menu shown below appears.

Add Bookmarks

To add a Bookmark from an open Web page:

- Display the Web page to add, go to Bookmarks on the Communicator menu and click Add Bookmark.

✔ *Netscape does not confirm that a bookmark has been added to the file.*

To create a Bookmark from the History list:

1. Click Communicator, History and select the listing to bookmark.

2. Right-click on your selection and choose Add To Bookmarks from the pop-up menu.

Delete Bookmarks

- Bookmarks may be deleted at anytime. For example, you may wish to delete a Bookmark if a Web site no longer exists or is no longer of interest to you.

To delete a Bookmark:

1. Click Communicator.

2. Click Bookmarks.

3. Click Edit Bookmarks.

4. In the Bookmarks window, select the Bookmark you want to delete by clicking on it from the Bookmark list.

5. Press the Delete key.

   OR

   Right-click on the Bookmark and select Delete Bookmark from the pop-up menu as shown in the following illustration.

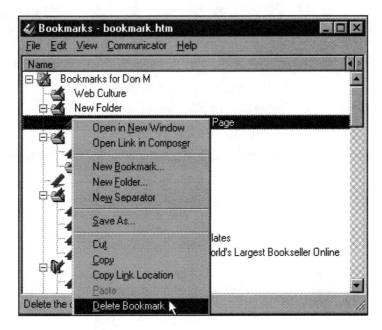

Print Web Pages

- You can print all information you find on the Internet.

To print a Web page:

✔ *Only displayed pages can be printed.*

1. Click the Print button on the Navigation toolbar.

   OR

   Click File, Print.

2. In the Print dialog box that displays, select the desired print options and click OK.

- In most cases, the Web page will be printed in the format shown in the Web page display.

Netscape Messenger: 4

◆ Start Netscape Messenger
◆ Configure Netscape Messenger
◆ Increase Font Size
◆ The Message List Window ◆ Get New Mail
◆ Read Messages ◆ Delete a Message
◆ Print Messages

Start Netscape Messenger

✔ *This section assumes that you have already set up an e-mail account with a service provider. If you do not have an e-mail address, contact your Internet Service Provider.*

■ Establishing a modem connection and configuring your computer to send and receive mail can be frustrating. Don't be discouraged. What follows are steps that will get you connected, but some of the information may have to be supplied by your Internet Service Provider. Calling for help will save you time and frustration.

• Click the Mailbox icon [icons] on the Component bar from the Navigator window.

OR

Start Netscape Messenger from the Netscape Communicator submenu on the Start, Programs menu.

KMMC-More Than Words ▶	Netscape Collabra
Microsoft Reference ▶	Netscape Composer
Movies Screen Saver ▶	Netscape Conference
Netscape 2.0 ▶	Netscape Messenger
Netscape Communicator ▶	Netscape Navigator

Configure Netscape Messenger

- Using Netscape Messenger you can send, receive, save, and print e-mail messages and attachments. First, you must configure the program with your e-mail account information.

- You may have already filled in this information if you completed the New Profile Setup Wizard when you installed Netscape Communicator.

- If not, follow these steps to get connected. You can also use these steps to change your e-mail setting.

Step 1: Identity Settings

- From the Navigator or Messenger menu:

  1. Click Edit and select Preferences.

  2. Double-click the Mail & Groups Category to display the list and click Identity.

  3. Enter your name, e-mail address, and any optional information in the Identity dialog boxes.

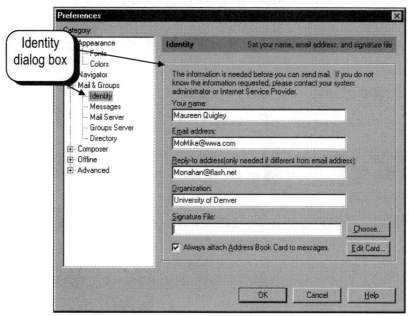

Step 2: Mail Server Preference Settings

- Completing this step will allow you to send and receive mail.

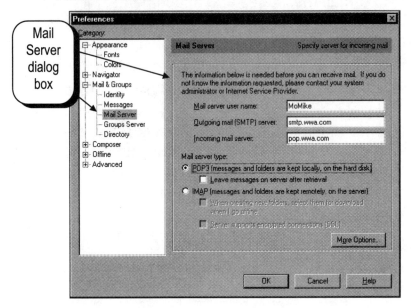

1. Click Mail Server from the Mail & Groups <u>C</u>ategory.

2. Enter your mail server user name. This is the part of your e-mail address that appears in front of the @ sign.

3. Enter your outgoing and incoming mail server address information.

   ✔ *Check with your ISP if you don't already have this information.*

4. Click [OK] to save and close the preference settings.

   ✔ *You should now be able to send and receive e-mail messages.*

Increase Font Size

- Netscape allows you to increase font size for larger text. When you increase the font size it affects all messages that you receive and send.

To increase font size:

1. Click <u>V</u>iew.

2. Click Increase <u>F</u>ont.

   ✔ *You can repeat the above steps until you find a size that you like.*

The Message List Window

- After you launch Messenger, a message list window will open, displaying the contents of the e-mail Inbox folder. You can retrieve, read, forward, and reply to messages from this window.

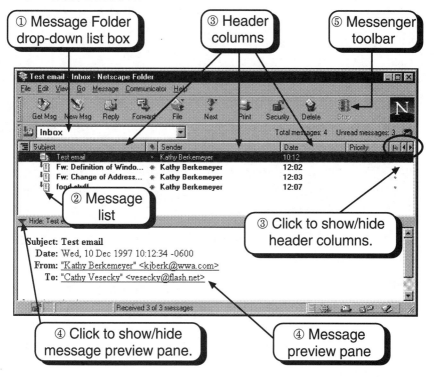

① Message Folder drop-down list box

③ Header columns

⑤ Messenger toolbar

② Message list

③ Click to show/hide header columns.

④ Click to show/hide message preview pane.

④ Message preview pane

- The message list window includes the following:

  ① The Message Folder drop-down list box displays the currently selected message folder. Click the down arrow to display a list of other message folders.

  ② The message list displays header information for each of the messages contained in the selected folder.

  ③ Header columns list the categories of information available for each message, such as subject, sender, and date.

  ④ The message preview pane displays the content of the message currently selected from the message list. You can show/hide the preview pane by clicking on the blue triangle icon in the bottom-left corner of the message list pane.

  ⑤ The Messenger toolbar displays buttons for activating commonly used commands. Note that each button contains an image and a word describing the function.

Messenger Toolbar Buttons and Functions

 Retrieves new mail from your Internet mail server and loads it into the Inbox message folder.

 Opens the Message Composition screen allowing you to compose new mail messages.

 Allows you to reply to the sender of an e-mail message or to the sender and all other recipients of the e-mail message.

 Forwards a message you have received to another address.

 Stores the current message in one of six Messenger default file folders or in a new folder that you create.

Selects and displays the next of the unread messages in your Inbox.

 Prints the displayed message.

 Displays the security status of a message.

 Deletes the selected message. Deleted messages are moved to the Trash folder.

Get New Mail

■ You must be connected to your ISP to access new e-mail messages.

To retrieve new messages:

1. Click the Get Msg button ⟨Get Msg⟩ on the Messenger toolbar. (If you do not know your e-mail password, contact your ISP.)

2. If you have not instructed Netscape Messenger to save your password, you will have to enter it in the Password Entry dialog box that follows.

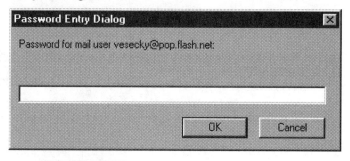

3. Click ⟨ OK ⟩.

- The Getting New Messages box opens, displaying the status of your message retrieval.

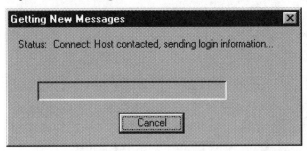

- Once your new messages are retrieved, they are listed in the message list window. By default, Messenger stores new mail messages in the Inbox folder.

To save your Password permanently in Messenger:

1. Click Edit, Preferences.

2. Click on Mail Server under the Mail & Groups Category to select it.

   ✔ *If the Mail & Groups menu is not displayed, expand the list by clicking the + sign next to the Mail & Groups category.*

3. Click the More Options button More Options... .

4. Select the Remember my mail password check box and click OK twice to save and exit Preferences.

Read Messages

- There are two ways to read messages:

  - You can read a message in the message preview pane located directly below the message list window. Single-click on a message from the message list and the contents of the message will appear in the preview pane.

✔ *If the message does not appear, the preview pane may be hidden. Click on the blue triangle icon at the bottom of the message list window to show the preview pane.*

OR

Double-click on the message from the message list to open it in its own window.

To close a message:

• Click File, Close.

OR

Click on the Close button (X) in the upper-right corner of the window.

To read the next unread message:

• Click the Next button on the Messenger toolbar.

OR

If you have reached the end of the current message, you can press the spacebar to proceed to the next unread message.

■ Once you have read a message, it remains stored in the Inbox folder until you delete it or file it in another folder. (See **Delete a Message** on page 22.)

✔ *You do not have to be online to read e-mail. You can reduce your online time by disconnecting from your ISP after retrieving your messages.*

✔ *Icons located to the left of message headers in the message list identify each message as either unread*

(retrieved during a previous Messenger session),

new *(and unread), or read* .

Delete a Message

- There are two steps required to delete a message permanently. Deleting a message from the message list moves the message to the Trash folder. You must then delete it from the Trash folder to remove it permanently from your hard disk.

  1. To delete a message, click on the message to select it from the message list window.

  2. Click the Delete button [Delete] on the Messenger toolbar.

To delete messages from the Trash folder:

- Click Empty Trash Folder from the File menu to delete all items stored there.

  OR

  Delete the desired message by selecting it and pressing the Delete key.

  ✔ *To select more than one message to delete, hold the Ctrl button while you click each message to delete. Once all the desired messages are selected, press the Delete key.*

Print Messages

- The message must first be open in order to print it.

  1. Click the Print button [Print] on the Messenger toolbar.

  2. In the Print dialog box that appears, select the desired print options and click [OK].

Netscape Messenger: 5

◆ New E-Mail Messages
◆ The Message Composition Toolbar
◆ Compose and Send Messages
◆ Reply to Mail ◆ Forward Mail
◆ Add Entries to the Personal Address Book
◆ Address a New Message Using the Personal
Address Book

New E-Mail Messages

- You can compose an e-mail message in Netscape Messenger on- or offline.

- After composing an e-mail message online, you have three choices:

  - send the message immediately

  - store the message in the Unsent Messages folder to be sent later (File, Send Later)

  - save the message in the Drafts folder to be finished and sent later (File, Save Draft)

- After composing a message offline (which frees up your phone line and also reduces any hourly ISP charges), store the message in your Unsent Messages folder until you are online and can send it.

The Message Composition Toolbar

■ The toolbar in the Message Composition window has several features that are specific only to the message composition screen.

Message Composition Toolbar Buttons and Functions

 Immediately sends current message.

 Used when replying to a message, the Quote feature allows you to include text from the original message.

 Select an address from the addresses stored in your personal Address Book to insert into address fields.

 By clicking the Attach button, you can send a file, a Web page, or your personal address card along with your e-mail message.

 Checks for spelling errors in the current message.

 Lets you save your message as a draft for later use.

 Sets the security status of a message.

 Stops the display of an HTML message or a message with an HTML attachment.

Compose and Send Messages

• There are four steps to composing and sending a basic e-mail message using Netscape Messenger:

Step 1: New Message

1. Click the New Message button 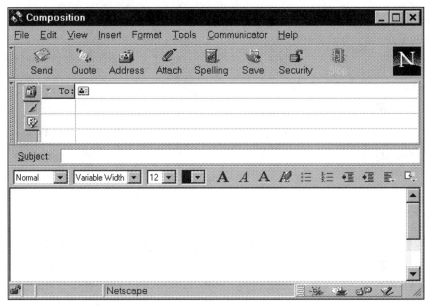 from the Messenger main screen.

    OR

    Press Ctrl+M.

    ✔ *The Message Composition window displays.*

2. In the Message Composition window, type the e-mail address(es) of the message recipient(s) in the To field.

    ✔ *If you are sending the message to multiple recipients, press Enter after typing each recipient's address to move to the next address line.*

    OR

    Click the Address button [Address] on the Message Composition toolbar and select an address to insert from the Address Book (see pages 30-32 for more information on using the Address Book).

- Click the To button ![To button] to display a drop-down menu of addressee options. Click on any of following options to enter the recipient information indicated:

To	The e-mail address of the person to whom the message is being sent.
CC (Carbon Copy)	The e-mail addresses of people who will receive copies of the message.
BCC (Blind Carbon Copy)	Same as CC, except these names will not appear anywhere in the message, so other recipients will not know that the person(s) listed in the BCC field received a copy.
Group	Names of Newsgroups that will receive this message (similar to Mail To). (See **Newsgroups** on page 201.)
Reply To	The e-mail address where replies should be sent.
Follow-up To	Another Newsgroup heading; used to identify Newsgroups to which comments should be posted (similar to Reply To).

Step 2: The Subject

- Click in the Subject field (or press Tab to move the cursor there) and type a banner for your message. This is the first thing the recipient will see announcing your e-mail message. The subject should be a few-word summation of your message.

Step 3: The Message

- Click to or Tab down to the blank composition area below the Subject field and type the body of your message.

To spell-check your e-mail message:

- Check the spelling of your message by clicking on the Spelling button ![Spelling] on the Message Composition toolbar and respond to the dialog prompts that follow.

Step 4: Sending the Message

To send a message immediately:

- Click the Send button ![Send] on the Message Composition toolbar.

To send a message later:

- Use these procedures to send message that you compose offline or that you wish to send later.

  ♦ Click File, Send Later.

  OR

  Click File, Save Draft.

- Saving the message in the Drafts folder lets you finish and then send it later.

Reply to Mail

■ Select the message from the message list or open the message in its own window:

1. Click the Reply button .

✔ *The Reply submenu displays*

2. Click Reply to Sender to reply to the original sender only.

   OR

   Select Reply to Sender and All Recipients to send a reply to the sender and all other recipients of the original message.

■ Selecting one of these options automatically inserts the recipient's name or e-mail address in the address fields.

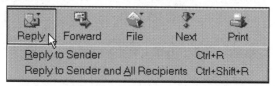

✔ *The Message Composition window opens, with the To, Cc, and Subject fields filled in for you.*

■ Compose your reply as you would a new message.

To include a copy of the original message with your reply:

1. Select the original message from the message list.

2. Click the New Msg button [New Msg] on the Messenger toolbar.

3. Click the Quote button [Quote] on the Message Composition toolbar.

   ✔ *The entire message will be automatically inserted in the body of your new message. You can edit the original message and header text as you wish.*

4. When you are finished, click the Send button [Send] to send the message immediately.

Forward Mail

■ To forward a message:

1. Select the message from the message list or open the message to forward.

2. Click the Forward button [Forward] from the toolbar.

   ✔ *The Message Composition window opens, with the Subject field filled in for you.*

   Subject [Fwd: Andy's Birthday Party]

3. Type the e-mail address of the new recipient in the To field.

   ✔ *If the original message does not appear in the composition area, click the Quote button [Quote] on the Message Composition toolbar to insert it.*

4. Click in the composition area and edit the message as desired. You can also type any additional text you want to include with the forwarded message.

5. When you are done, click the Send button [Send] to send the message immediately.

   OR

   Select File, Send Later to store the message in the Unsent Messages mailbox to be sent later.

   OR

   To save the reply as a draft to be edited and sent later, select Save Draft from the File menu.

Add Entries to the Personal Address Book

■ You can compile a personal Address Book to store e-mail addresses that you use often. Click on entries from the Address Book to insert an e-mail address automatically into the e-mail message header.

To add a name to the Address Book:

1. Click Communicator, Address Book.

   ✔ *The Address Book window displays.*

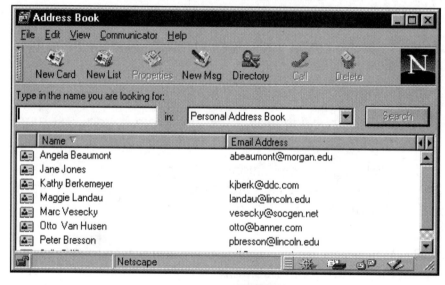

2. Click the New Card button ![New Card] on the Address Book toolbar.

3. In the New Card box that appears, enter the recipient's first name, last name, organization, title, and e-mail address.

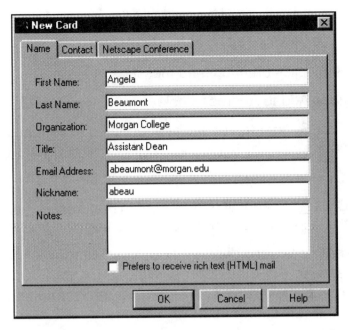

- In the Nickname field, if desired, type a unique nickname for the recipient. When addressing a message, you can use the recipient's nickname in the To field and Messenger will automatically fill in the full e-mail address.

- In the Notes field, type any notes you want to store about the recipient.

- Click the Contact tab, if desired, and enter the recipient's postal address and phone number.

4. Click .

■ You can edit an address book entry at any time by double-clicking on the person's name in the Address Book window.

■ To add the name and address of the sender of a message you are reading:

- Click Message, Add to Address Book.

Add a name to the Address Book from the Add to Address Book submenu:

1. Right-click on unopened message.

2. Click Add to Address Book.

3. Click Sender to add the sender name to your address book.

   OR

   Click All to add all names from the addressee fields to the Address Book (e.g., everyone from the cc: field).

- The New Card dialog box opens, with the sender's name and e-mail address filled in for you. You can enter a nickname and any other information you want in the remaining fields.

Address a New Message Using the Personal Address Book

1. Click the New Msg button New Msg to open the Message Composition window.

2. Click on the Address button Address on the Message Composition toolbar and select a recipient(s) from the list in the Address Book window.

3. Double-click on the name from the list of addresses.

4. Click OK to close the Address Book. The name(s) are automatically inserted in the address field.

Netscape Messenger: 6

◆ Attached Files ◆ View File Attachments
◆ Save Attached Files
◆ Attach Files to Messages

Attached Files

■ Sometimes an e-mail message will come with a separate file(s) attached. Messages containing attachments are indicated when you display a message and it contains a paperclip icon to the right of the message header. Attachments can be used when you want to send someone a document, a spreadsheet, a video clip, or any other type of file.

■ With Messenger, you can view both plain text attachments and binary attachments. Binary files are files containing more than plain text (i.e., images, sound clips, and formatted text, such as spreadsheets and word processor documents).

■ Almost any e-mail program can read plain text files. Binary files, however, must be decoded by the receiving e-mail program before they can be displayed in a readable form. When a binary attachment arrives, Messenger automatically recognizes and decodes it.

View File Attachments

■ E-mail attachments are displayed in one of two ways.

View attachments Inline:

- If you select <u>V</u>iew, <u>A</u>ttachments, <u>I</u>nline, you see the attachment in a separate attachment window below the message. If there is more than one attachment, you will see a series of sequential windows—one with the message and the other with the attachments.

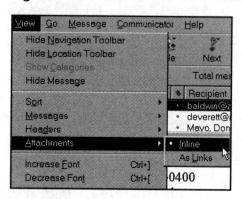

✔ *Only plain text, images, and Web page attachments can be viewed Inline.*

View attachments As Links:

- If you select <u>V</u>iew, <u>A</u>ttachments, As <u>L</u>inks, the window below the message displays an attachment box listing the details of the attachment. It also serves as a link to the attachment.

✔ *Viewing attachments as links reduces the time it takes to open a message on screen.*

- Click on the blue-highlighted text in the attachment box to display the attachment.

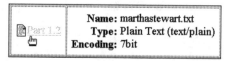

■ You can right-click on the attachment icon portion of the attachment box to display a menu of mail options such as forwarding, replying, or deleting the message.

- By right-clicking on the actual attachment, you can choose from several save options.

- If you open a Web page attachment while online, you will connect to that Web site. If you are not online, the Web page will display fully formatted, but it will not be active.

■ If an attached image displays as a link even after you select View, Attachments, Inline, it is probably because it is an image type that Messenger does not recognize. In this case, you need to install and/or open a plug-in or program with which to view the unrecognized image.

Save Attached Files

■ You can save an attached file to your hard drive or disk for future use or reference.

To save an attachment:

1. Open the message containing the attachment to save.

2. If the attachment is in Inline view, convert it to a link (View, Attachments, As Links).

3. Right-click on the link and select Save Link As.

   OR

   Click on the link to open the attachment. Select File, Save As, or, if Messenger does not recognize the attachment's file type, click the Save File button in the Unknown File Type dialog box.

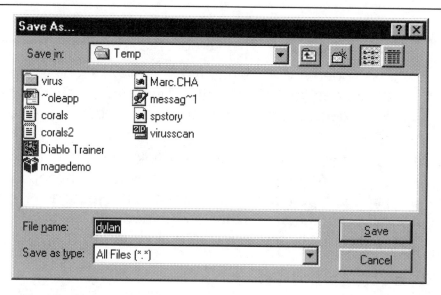

4. In the Save As dialog box that follows, click the Save in drop-down list box and select the drive and folder in which to save the file.

5. Click in the File name text box and type a name for the file.

6. Click Save.

Attach Files to Messages

- Any type of file can be sent as an attachment to an e-mail message—including text files, graphics, spreadsheets, and HTML documents.

To attach a file to an e-mail message:

1. Click the Attach button Attach on the Message Composition toolbar, and select File from the drop-down menu that appears.

2. In the Enter file to attach dialog box that follows, click the Look in drop-down list box and select the drive and folder containing the file to attach.

3. Then select the file to attach and click Open.

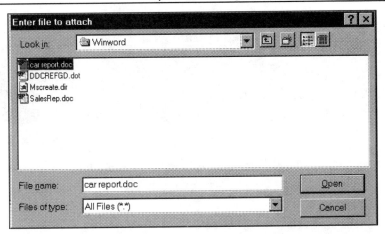

- After you have attached a file, the Attachments field in the Mail Composition window displays the name and location of the attached file.

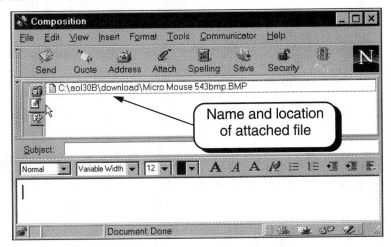

✔ *Messages containing attachments usually take longer to send than those without attachments. When attaching very large files or multiple files, you may want to zip (compress) the files before attaching them. To do so, both you and the recipient need a file compression program, such as WinZip or PKZip.*

- Once you have attached the desired files and finished composing your message, you can send the e-mail, save it in the Unsent Messages folder for later delivery, or save it as a draft for later editing.

Microsoft Internet Explorer: 7

◆ Start Internet Explorer 4 ◆ Change Font Size
◆ Internet Explorer Screen
◆ Exit Internet Explorer

Start Internet Explorer 4

- When you first install Internet Explorer and you are using the Active Desktop, you may see the message illustrated below when you turn on your computer. If you are familiar with Explorer 3, you may want to select 1 to learn the new features in Explorer 4. Select 2 to learn about Channels.

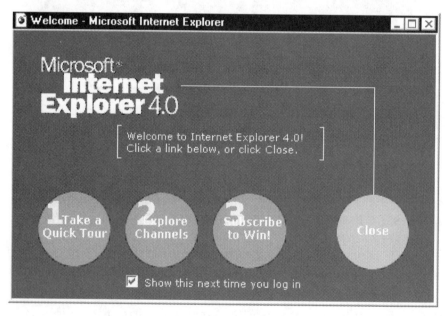

To start Internet Explorer:

- Click on the Desktop.

  OR

  Click 🝙 on the Taskbar.

  OR

  Click the Start button 🝙 **Start**, then select Programs, Internet Explorer, and click Internet Explorer.

Change Font Size

- Internet Explorer allows you to increase the font size for on screen text.

To increase font size:

1. Click View.

2. Click Fonts.

3. Select:

   - Largest

     OR

     Larger

Internet Explorer Screen

- When you connect to the World Wide Web, the first screen that displays is called a home page. The home page is the first page of any World Wide Web site.

- You can change the first page that you see when you connect to Explorer.

To change the home page:

1. Click View, Internet Options.

2. Enter a new address in the Address text box.

   ✔ *The page that you see when you are connected may differ from the one illustrated below.*

3. Click [OK].

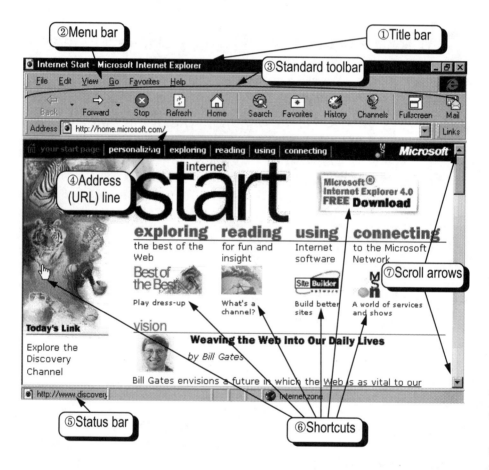

① **Title bar**   Displays the name of the program and the current Web page. You can minimize, restore, or close Explorer using the buttons on the right side of the Title bar.

② **Menu bar**   Displays menus currently available, which provide drop-down lists of commands for executing Internet Explorer tasks.

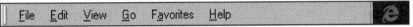

    The Internet Explorer button on the right side of the Menu bar rotates when action is occurring or information is being processed.

③ **Standard toolbar**   Displays frequently used commands.

④ **Address (URL) line**   Displays the address of the current page. You can click here, type a new address, press Enter, and go to a new location (if it's an active Web site). You can also start a search from this line.

The Links bar contains links to various Microsoft sites. Drag the split bar to the left or somewhere else on the screen to display current Links. You can add or delete links.

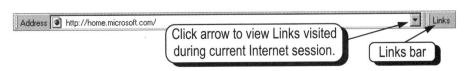

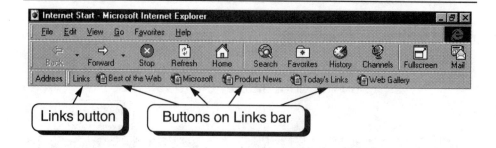

Links button

Buttons on Links bar

⑤ **Status bar** Displays information about actions occurring on the page and the Security Level. Internet Security Properties lets you control content that is downloaded on to your computer.

⑥ **Shortcuts** Click on shortcuts (also called hyperlinks) to move to other Web sites. Shortcuts are usually easy to recognize. They can be underlined text, text of different colors, "buttons" of various sizes and shapes, or graphics. You are pointing to a shortcut when the mouse pointer changes to a hand, and the full name of the Web site appears on the Status bar.

⑦ **Scroll arrows** Scroll arrows are used to move the screen view, as in all Windows applications.

Exit Internet Explorer

■ Exiting Internet Explorer and disconnecting from your service provider are two separate steps. It is important to remember that if you close Internet Explorer (or any other browser), you must also disconnect (or hang up) from your service provider. If you don't disconnect, you'll continue incurring any applicable charges.

Microsoft Internet Explorer: 8

◆ Standard Toolbar Buttons
◆ Open a Web Site from the Address Bar

Standard Toolbar Buttons

- The Internet Explorer Standard toolbar displays frequently used commands. If the Standard toolbar is *not* visible when you start Explorer, open the View menu, select Toolbars, then select Standard Buttons.

Internet Explorer Toolbar and Functions

 Moves back through pages previously displayed. Back is available only if you have moved around among Web pages in the current Explorer session.

 Moves forward through pages previously displayed. Forward is available only if you have used the Back button.

 Interrupts the opening of a page that is taking too long to display.

 Reloads the current page.

 Returns you to your home page. You can change your home page to open to any Web site or a blank page (View, Internet Options, General).

 Allows you to select from a number of search services with a variety of options.

Displays the Web sites that you have stored or bookmarked using the Favorites menu.

 Displays links to Web sites that you have visited in previous days and weeks. You can change the number of days that sites are stored in your History folder (View, Internet Options, General).

 Displays the list of current channels on the Explorer bar.

 Conceals Menu, titles, Status bar, and Address bar to maximize your screen for viewing a Web page. Click it again to restore your screen.

 Displays a drop-down menu with various Mail and News options. You will learn about Outlook Express e-mail options in Chapters 10-12.

Open a Web Site from the Address Bar

1. Click in the Address bar and start typing the address of the Web site you want to open.

2. If you have visited the site before, Internet Explorer will try to complete the address automatically. If it is the correct address, press Enter to go to it. If it is not the correct address, type over the suggested address that displayed on the line.

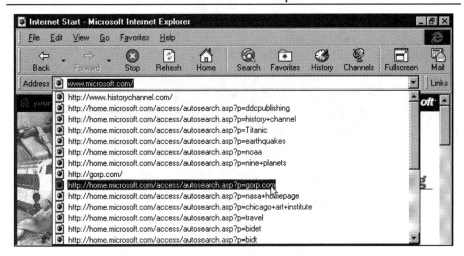

✔ *To turn off the AutoComplete feature, open the View menu, select Internet Options, and click the Advanced tab. Deselect Use AutoComplete in the Browsing area of the dialog box.*

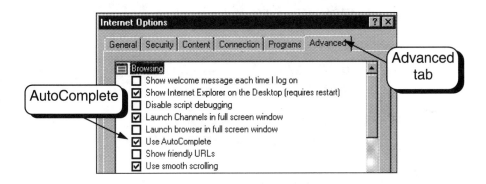

Microsoft Internet Explorer: 9

◆ Open and Add to the Favorites Folder
◆ Open Web Sites from the Favorites Folder
◆ Create New Folders in the Favorites Folder
◆ AutoSearch from the Address Bar

Open and Add to the Favorites Folder

- As you spend more time exploring Web sites, you will find sites that you want to visit frequently. You can store shortcuts to these sites in the Favorites folder.

To add a site to the Favorites folder:

1. Go to the desired Web site.

2. Open the Favorites menu or right-click anywhere on the page and select Add To Favorites.

   ✔ *The Add Favorite dialog box appears*

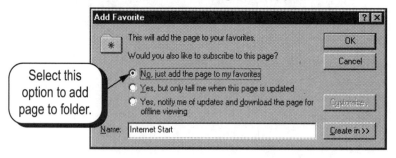

3. The name of the Page you have opened appears in the Name box. You may also choose to subscribe to a page. Subscribing to a page means you can schedule automatic updates to that site. Choose from the following options:

   ♦ No, just add the page to my favorites.

   ✔ *Choose this option to put a shortcut to the Web site in your Favorites folder.*

   ♦ Yes, but only tell me when this page is updated.

   ✔ *Explorer will alert you when an update to the site is available.*

   ♦ Yes, notify me of updates and download the page for offline viewing

   ✔ *Explorer will automatically download and update to your computer.*

4. Click `OK` to add the Web address to the Favorites folder.

Open Web Sites from the Favorites Folder

■ Click the Favorites button `Favorites` on the Standard toolbar to open Web sites from the Favorites folder. The Explorer bar will open on the left side of the Browser window.

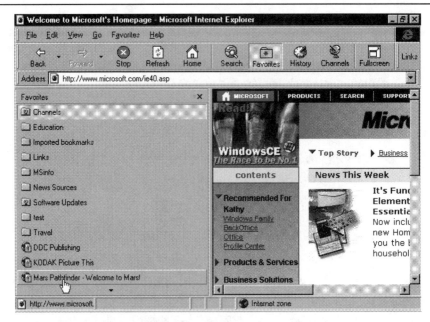

- Click on an address or open a folder and select a site. Close the Explorer bar by clicking the Close button ☒ or

  the Favorites button 🔖 Favorites on the toolbar.

- You can also open the Favorites menu and select a site from the list or from a folder.

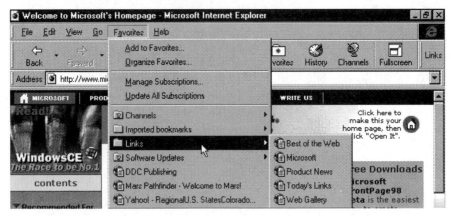

Create New Folders in the Favorites Folder

- You can create new folders before or after you have saved addresses in your Favorites folder.

To create a new folder:

1. Click Favorites and select Organize Favorites.

2. Click the Create New Folder button [icon].

3. Type the name of the new folder and press Enter.

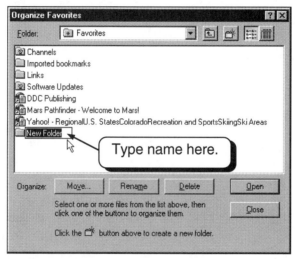

AutoSearch from the Address Bar

- In addition to displaying and entering addresses in the Address bar, you can use AutoSearch to perform a quick search directly from the Address bar.
- Click once in the Address bar and type *go, find,* or *?* and press the spacebar once. Enter the word or phrase you want to find and press Enter. For example, if you want to search for information about the year 2000, type *find the year 2000* on the Address bar and press Enter.

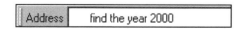

Outlook Express: 10

◆ Start Outlook Express
◆ Configure Outlook Express
◆ Outlook Express Main Window
◆ Retrieve New Messages ◆ The Mail Window
◆ Read Messages ◆ Delete a Message
◆ Print a Message ◆ Save a Message

Start Outlook Express

- Click the Mail icon on the Taskbar.

  OR

  Click <u>G</u>o, <u>M</u>ail.

✔ *Clicking the Mail icon from the Explorer main window may take you to the Microsoft Outlook organizational program. To use the more compact Outlook Express as your default mail program, click <u>V</u>iew, Internet <u>O</u>ptions from the Explorer main window. Click the Programs tab and choose Outlook Express from the <u>M</u>ail pull-down menu.*

✔ *If you downloaded Internet Explorer 4, be sure that you downloaded the standard version, which includes Outlook Express in addition to the Web browser.*

Configure Outlook Express

✔ *This section assumes that you have already set up an e-mail account with a service provider.*

- Establishing a modem connection and configuring your computer to send and receive mail can be frustrating. Don't be discouraged. What follows are steps that will get you connected, but some of the information may have to be supplied by your Internet Service Provider.

- Before you can use Outlook Express to send and receive e-mail, you must configure the program with your e-mail account information.

- You may have already filled in this information if you completed the Internet Connection Wizard when you started Internet Explorer for the first time. If not, you can enter the information by running the Internet Connection Wizard again.

Using Internet Connection Wizard

1. Launch Outlook Express.

2. Open the Tools menu, select Accounts.

3. Click the Mail tab.

4. Click Add and select Mail to start the Connection Wizard.

   ✔ *The Internet Connection Wizard will ask for information necessary to set up or add an e-mail account.*

5. Enter the name you want to appear on the "From" line in your outgoing messages. Click Next.

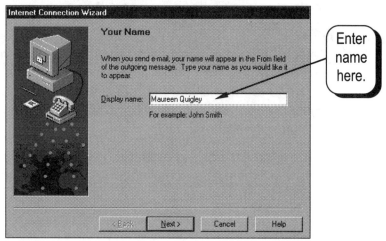

6. Type your e-mail address. This is the address that people use to send mail to you. Click Next.

7. Enter the names of your incoming and outgoing mail servers. Check with your Internet Service Provider if you do not know what they are. Click Next.

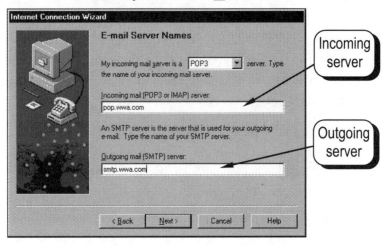

8. Enter the logon name and password that your ISP requires for you to access your mail. Again, if you are not sure about this information, contact your ISP. Click Next.

9. Enter a name for your e-mail account. The name you enter will appear when you open the Accounts list on the Tools menu in Outlook Express. It can be any name that you choose. Click Next.

10. Select the type of connection you are using to reach the Internet. If you are connecting through a phone line, you will need to have a dial-up connection. If you have an existing connection, click Next and select from the list of current connections.

11. Select Use an existing dial-up connection, or select Create a new dial-up connection and follow the directions to create a new one.

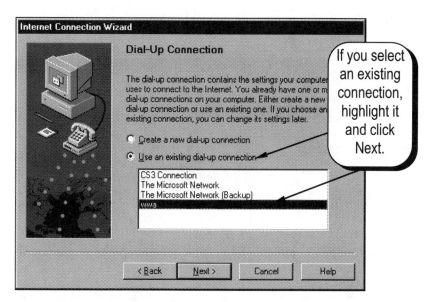

12. If you select <u>U</u>se an existing dial-up connection, click Finish in the last window to save the settings.

✔ *You should then be able to launch Outlook Express and send and receive mail and attachments.*

Outlook Express Main Window

■ After you launch Outlook Express, the main Outlook Express window opens by default. You can access any e-mail function from this window.

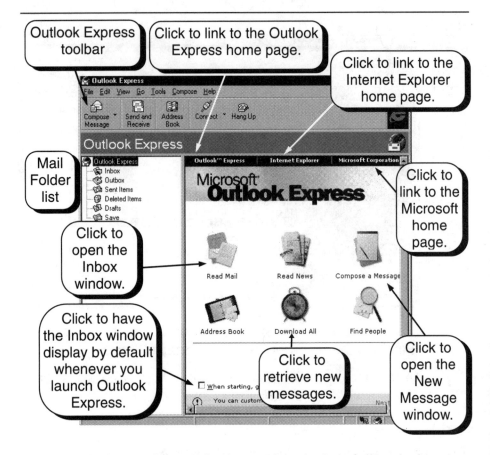

Outlook Express toolbar

Click to link to the Outlook Express home page.

Click to link to the Internet Explorer home page.

Mail Folder list

Click to link to the Microsoft home page.

Click to open the Inbox window.

Click to have the Inbox window display by default whenever you launch Outlook Express.

Click to retrieve new messages.

Click to open the New Message window.

- Descriptions of items in the main window follow below:

  - The Mail Folder list displays in the left column of the window, with the Outlook Express main folder selected. To view the contents of a different folder, click on the desired folder in the folder list.

  - Shortcuts to different e-mail functions are located in the center of the window. Click on a shortcut to access the indicated task or feature.

  - Hyperlinks to Microsoft home pages are located at the top of the window. Click on a link to connect to the indicated home page.

- The Outlook Express toolbar displays buttons for commonly used commands. Note that each button contains an image and text that describes the button function. Clicking any of these buttons will activate the indicated task immediately.

Retrieve New Messages

- You can retrieve new mail from any Outlook Express window.

1. Click the Send and Receive button ![Send and Receive] on the toolbar.

2. In the Connection dialog box that displays, enter your ISP user name in the User Name text box and your password in the Password text box. Click [OK]. (If you do not know your user name or password, contact your ISP.)

✔ *You must re-enter your password each time you reconnect to the Internet unless you set Outlook Express to save your password permanently. To do so, select the Save Password check box in the connection dialog box and click OK.*

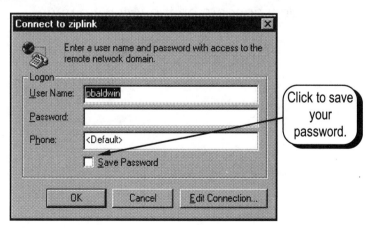

3. Once you are connected to the Internet and Outlook Express is connected to your ISP mail server, new mail messages will begin downloading from your ISP mail server.

✔ *A dialog box displays the status of your retrieval.*

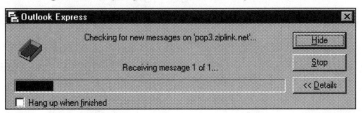

The Mail Window

- After retrieving new messages, Outlook Express stores them in the Inbox folder.

- To view your new messages, you must open the Mail window and display the contents of the Inbox folder.

1. Click the Read Mail shortcut [Read Mail] in the Outlook Express main window.

2. The Mail window opens with the Inbox folder displayed. A description of the items in the Mail window appears on the following page.

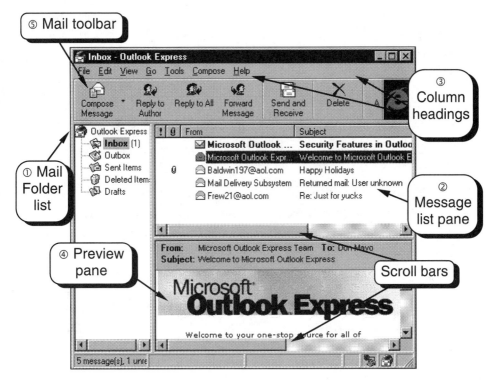

⑤ Mail toolbar

③ Column headings

① Mail Folder list

② Message list pane

④ Preview pane

Scroll bars

✔ *In the message list, unread messages are displayed in bold text with a sealed envelope icon ☒. Messages that have been read are listed in regular text with an open envelope icon ◳.*

① The Mail Folder list displays the currently selected message folder, the contents of which are displayed in the mail list. Click on another folder to display its contents in the mail list.

② The message list pane displays a header for each of the messages contained in the currently selected mail folder.

③ Column headings list the categories of information included in each message header, such as subject, from, and date received.

④ The preview pane displays the content of the message currently selected from the message list. You can show/hide the preview pane by selecting View, Layout and clicking on the Use preview pane check box.

⑤ The Mail toolbar displays command buttons for working with messages. These commands vary depending on the message folder currently displayed (Inbox, Sent, Outbox, etc.).

Read Messages

✔ *You do not have to be online to read e-mail. You can reduce your online time if you disconnect from your ISP after retrieving your messages and read them offline.*

■ You must have the Mail window open and the mail folder containing the message to read displayed.

To read messages:

• To read a message in the preview pane, click on the desired message header in the message list. If the message does not appear, select View, Layout, Use preview pane.

OR

To open and read a message in a separate window, double-click on the desired message header in the message list.

✔ *The Message window opens displaying the Message toolbar and the contents of the selected message.*

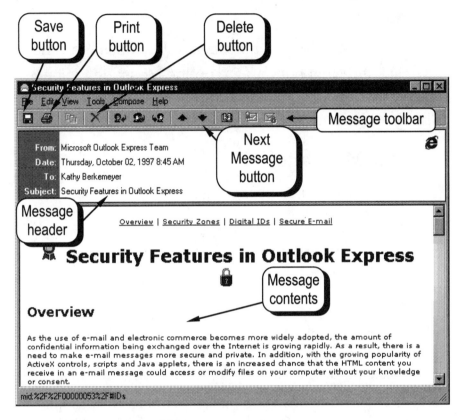

To close the Message window:

- Click File, Close.

OR

Click on the Close button (X) in the upper-right corner of the window.

✔ *Use the scroll bars in the Message window or the preview pane to view hidden parts of a displayed message. Or, press the down arrow key to scroll down through the message.*

To read the next unread message:

- Select View, Next, Next Unread Message.

  OR

  If you are viewing a message in the Message window, click the Next button ▼ on the Message toolbar.

- Once you have read a message, it remains stored in the Inbox folder until you delete it or file it in another folder.

Delete a Message

1. Select the desired header from the message list in the Mail window.

2. Click the Delete button ✕ Delete in the Mail toolbar, or select Edit, Delete.

   OR

1. Open the desired message in the Message window.

2. Click the Delete button ✕ on the Message toolbar.

✔ *To select more than one message from the message list to delete, press the Ctrl button while you click each message header.*

Print a Message

1. Select the message you want to print from the message list in the Mail window or open the message in the Message window.

2. Select Print from the File menu.

3. In the Print dialog box that opens, select the desired print options and click OK.

- You can send the message to the printer using the most recently used print settings by opening the message in the Message window and clicking the Print button on the Message toolbar.

Save a Message

1. Open the desired message in the Message window and click the Save button 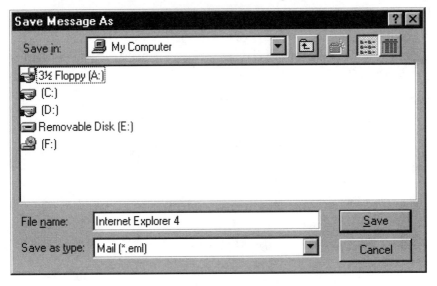 on the Message toolbar.

2. In the Save Message As dialog box that opens, click the Save in drop-down list box and select the drive and folder in which to store the message file.

3. Click in the File name box and enter a name for the message.

4. Click Save.

Outlook Express: 11

◆ Compose New Messages ◆ Send Messages
◆ Reply to Mail ◆ Forward Mail
◆ Add Entries to the Personal Address Book
◆ Address a New Message Using the Personal
Address Book

Compose New Messages

- You can compose an e-mail message in Outlook Express online or offline. When composing an e-mail message online, you can send the message immediately after creating it.

- When composing a message offline, you will need to store the message in your Outbox folder until you are online and can send it. (See **Send Messages** on page 63.)

To create a message:

1. Open the New Message window.

2. Click the Compose Message button on the toolbar in either the Mail window or the Main window.

   ✔ *The New Message window displays.*

3. In the New Message window, type the e-mail address(es) of the message recipient(s) in the To field.

   ✔ *If you type the first few characters of a name or e-mail address that is saved in your Address Book, Outlook Express will automatically complete it for you.*

   OR

   Click the Index Card icon in the To field or the

   Address Book button on the New Message toolbar

and select an address to insert from your personal Address Book. (See page 68 for information on using the Address Book.)

✔ *If you are sending the message to multiple recipients, insert a comma or semicolon between each recipient's address.*

4. After inserting the address(es) in the To field, you may click in either of the following fields and enter the recipient information indicated:

CC (Carbon Copy)	The e-mail addresses of people who will receive copies of the message.
BCC (Blind Carbon Copy)	Same as CC, except these names will not appear anywhere in the message, so other recipients will not know that the person(s) listed in the BCC field received a copy.

5. Click in the Subject field and type the subject of the message. An entry in this field is required.

6. Type your message in the blank composition area below the Subject field.

✔ *You can check the spelling of your message by selecting Spelling from the Tools menu and responding to the prompts that follow.*

Send Messages

■ Once you have created a message, you have three choices:

- to send the message immediately
- to store the message in the Outbox folder to be sent later
- to save the message in the Drafts folder to be edited and sent later

To send a message immediately:

✔ *In order to send messages immediately, you must first select Options from the Tools menu in the Mail window. Then click on the Send tab and select the Send messages immediately check box. If this option is not selected, clicking the Send button will not send a message immediately, but will send the message to your Outbox until you perform the Send and Receive task.*

1. Click the Send button [Send] on the New Message toolbar.

   OR

   Click File, Send Message.

2. Outlook Express then connects to your ISP's mail server and sends out the new message. If the connection to the mail server is successful, the sending mail icon displays in the lower-right corner of the status bar until the transmittal is complete.

- Sometimes, however, Outlook Express cannot immediately connect to the mail server and instead has to store the new message in the Outbox for later delivery. When this happens, the sending mail icon does not appear, and the number next to your Outbox folder increases by one [Outbox (1)].

- Outlook Express does not automatically reattempt to send a message after a failed connection. Instead, you need to send the message manually from the Outbox (see **To send messages from your Outbox folder** below).

To store a message in your Outbox folder for later delivery:

1. Select File, Send Later in the New Message window.

   ✔ *The Send Mail prompt displays, telling you that the message will be stored in our Outbox folder.*

2. Click [OK].

   ✔ *The message is saved in the Outbox.*

To send messages from your Outbox folder:

- Click on the Send and Receive button [Send and Receive] on the toolbar.

   OR

   Click Tools, Send and Receive, All Accounts.

   ✔ *When you use the Send and Receive command, Outlook Express sends out all messages stored in the Outbox and automatically downloads any new mail messages from the mail server.*

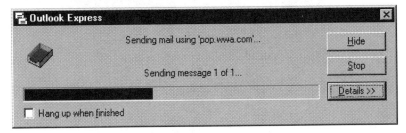

Reply to Mail

- In Outlook Express, you can reply to a message automatically, without having to enter the recipient's name or e-mail address.

- When replying, you have a choice of replying to the author and all recipients of the original message or to the author only.

To reply to the author and all recipients:

1. Select the message you want to reply to from the message list in the Mail window.

2. Click the Reply to All button ![Reply to All] on the Mail toolbar.

To reply to the author only:

- Click the Reply to Author button ![Reply to Author] on the Mail toolbar.

- Once you have selected a reply command, the New Message window opens with the address fields and the Subject filled in for you.

   ✔ *You can access all of the mail send commands by right-clicking on the message in the Message list.*

- The original message is automatically included in the body of your response. To turn off this default insertion, select Options from the Tools menu, click on the Send tab, deselect the Include message in reply check box, and click OK.

- To compose your reply, click in the composition area and type your text as you would in a new message.

- When you are done, click the Send button ▣Send on the New Message toolbar to send the message immediately. Or, select Send Later from the File menu to store the message in the Outbox folder for later delivery. To save the reply as a draft to be edited and sent later, select Save from the File menu.

Forward Mail

- There are times when you will want to forward mail that you have received.

  1. Select the message to forward from the message list in the Mail window.

  2. Click the Forward Message button ⬛ on the Mail toolbar.

     ✔ *The New Message window opens with the original message displayed and the Subject field filled in for you.*

  3. Fill in the e-mail address information by either typing each address or selecting the recipients from your Address Book. (See **Address a New Message Using the Personal Address Book** on page 70.)

     ✔ *If you are forwarding the message to multiple recipients, insert a comma or semicolon between each recipient's address.*

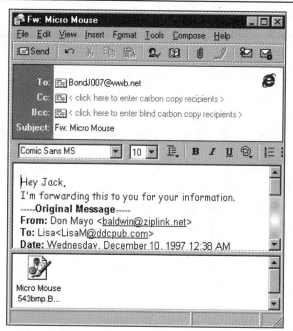

4. Click in the composition area and type any text you wish to send with the forwarded message.

5. When you are done, click the Send button ⌐⊟Send on the New Message toolbar to send the message immediately.

OR

Select Send Later from the File menu to store the message in the Outbox folder for later delivery.

Add Entries to the Personal Address Book

- In Outlook Express, you can use the Windows Address Book to store e-mail addresses. You can then use the Address Book to find and automatically insert addresses when creating new messages.

To add an entry to the Address Book:

1. Click the Address Book button ⊞Address Book on the toolbar in the Mail window or the Main window.

68

✔ *The Address Book window opens.*

2. Click the New Contact button ![New Contact] on the Address Book toolbar.

✔ *The Contact Properties dialog box displays.*

3. In the Properties dialog box, type the First, Middle, and Last names of the new contact in the appropriate text boxes.

4. Type the contact's e-mail address in the Add new text box and then click the Add button.

✔ *You can repeat this procedure if you wish to list additional e-mail addresses for the contact.*

5. In the Nickname text box, you can enter a unique nickname for the contact.

✔ *When addressing a new message, you can type the nickname in the To field, rather than typing the entire address, and Outlook Express will automatically complete the address.*

To add an Address Book entry from an e-mail message:

- You can automatically add the name and address of the sender of a message.

  1. Open the message in the Message window.

  2. Right-click on the sender's name in the To field.

  3. Select Add to Address Book from the shortcut menu.

- You can also set Outlook Express to add the address of recipients automatically when you reply to a message.

- Select <u>O</u>ptions from the <u>T</u>ools menu and select the <u>A</u>utomatically put people I reply to in my Address Book check box on the General tab.

✔ *You can edit an Address Book entry at any time by double-clicking on the person's name in the contact list in the Address Book window.*

Address a New Message Using the Personal Address Book

1. Click the Select Recipients button 📖 on the New Message toolbar.

2. In the Select Recipients dialog box that follows, select the address to insert from the contact list.

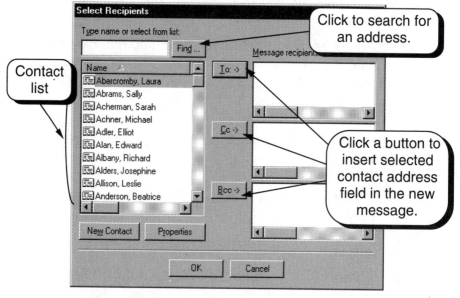

3. Click the button for the field in which you want to insert the address (<u>T</u>o, <u>C</u>c, or <u>B</u>cc).

4. Click [OK] to return to the New Message window when you are finished.

Outlook Express: 12

◆ View Attached Files ◆ Save Attached Files
◆ Attach Files to a Message

View Attached Files

- Sometimes e-mail messages come with separate files attached. Messages containing attachments show a paperclip icon ▯ to the left of the message header.

- If the selected message is displayed in the preview pane, a larger paper clip attachment icon will appear to the right of the header at the top of the preview pane.

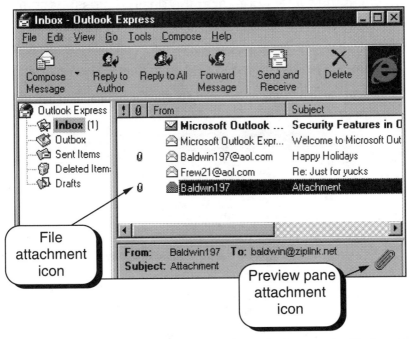

- If you open the selected message in its own window, an attachment icon will appear in a separate pane below the message.

Attachment icon

To view an attachment:

1. Open the folder containing the desired message in the Mail window.

2. Select the message containing the desired attachment(s) from the message list to display it in the preview pane.

✔ *If the attachment is an image, it will display in the message.*

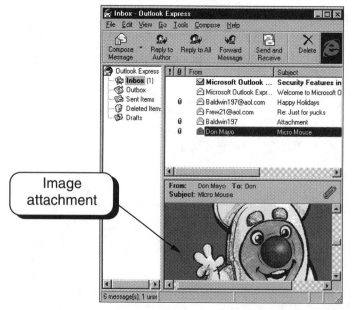

Image attachment

✔ *If the image does not display, click Tools, Options, click the Read tab, select the Automatically show picture attachments in messages check box, and click OK.*

■ Other types of attachments, such as programs, word processor documents, or media clips, do not display in the message, but have to be opened in a separate window.

To open an attachment in a separate window:

1. Click on the attachment icon 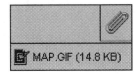 in the preview pane. A button will display with the file name and size of the attachment.

2. Click on this button.

3. If the Open Attachment Warning dialog box displays, select the desired option and click ☐ OK ☐.

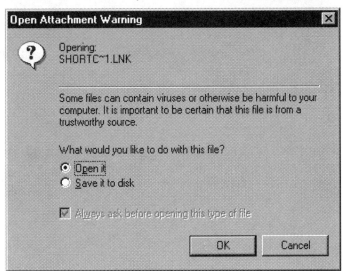

✔ *If you are not sure of the source of the attachment, you may want to save the attachment to a disk and run it through an anti-virus program.*

- Outlook Express will open the attached file or play the attached media clip.

- If the attached file does not open, Outlook Express does not recognize the file type of the attached file. Your computer may not contain the necessary plug-in or application to view it.

- To view an unrecognized attachment, you have to install and/or open the application or plug-in needed to view it.

Save Attached Files

- If desired, you can save an attached file to your hard drive or disk for future use or reference.

To save an attachment:

1. Select Save Attachments from the File menu, and select the attachment to save from the submenu that displays.

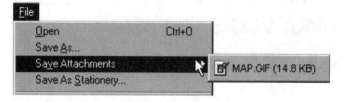

OR

Right-click on the attachment icon in the Message window and select the Save As option.

2. In the Save As dialog box that follows, click the Save in drop-down list box and select the drive and folder in which to save the file.

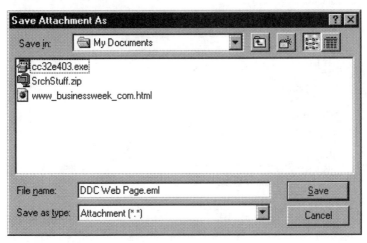

3. Click in the File name text box and type a name for the file.

4. Click Save.

Attach Files to a Message

- You can attach a file to an e-mail message.

  ✔ *When attaching very large files or multiple files, you may want to zip (compress) the files before attaching them. To do so, both you and the recipient need a file compression program, such as WinZip or PKZip.*

To add an attachment:

1. Click the Insert File button [📎] on the New Message toolbar.

OR

Click Insert, File Attachment.

2. In the Insert Attachment dialog box that appears, click the Look in drop-down list box and select the drive and folder containing the file to attach. Then select the file and click Attach.

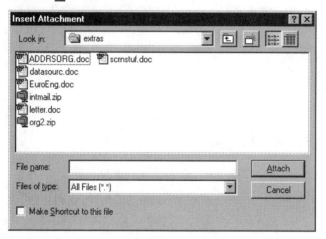

✔ *The attachment will appear as an icon in the body of the message.*

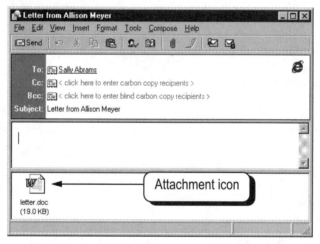

✔ *You can add multiple attachments by repeating the procedure as many times as you like.*

✔ *Before you send a message containing an attachment, you should make sure the recipient's e-mail program can read the attachment.*

America Online: 13

◆ About America Online ◆ Start America Online 4.0
◆ The AOL Home Page, Menu, and Toolbar
◆ Change Font Size ◆ AOL Help ◆ Exit AOL

About America Online

- America Online (AOL) is an all-purpose online service. Unlike Netscape Navigator or Microsoft Internet Explorer, AOL is not an Internet browser, yet you can browse the Internet using AOL navigation features.

- Unlike Internet browsers, AOL does not require a separate Internet Service Provider for Internet access, nor does it require a separate mail server connection to access e-mail from the AOL Mail Center.

Start America Online 4.0

1. Click the AOL icon ▲ on your desktop. This icon should display on your desktop after you install AOL.

   OR

   Click the Start button 🪟 Start, Programs, America Online, America Online 4.0.

2. Make sure your screen name is displayed in the Select Screen Name box and type your password in the Enter Password box.

3. Click the Sign On button SIGN ON to connect to the AOL server.

The AOL Home Page, Menu, and Toolbar

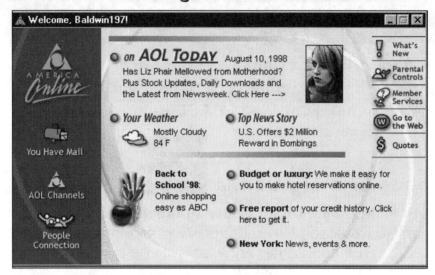

- After you log on to America Online, you will see a series of screens. The final first screen you see is the AOL home page or start page. The AOL home page contains links to daily AOL featured areas and constant AOL areas such as *Channels* and *What's New*. You can also access your mailbox from the home page.

- The AOL menu displays currently available options. Click the menu item to display a drop-down list of links to AOL areas and basic filing, editing, and display options.

- The AOL toolbar contains buttons for AOL's most commonly used commands. Choosing a button activates the indicated task immediately.

	You have new mail if the flag on the mailbox is in the up position. Click to display your mailbox.
	Click to compose new mail messages.
	Click to read new, old, or sent mail; to set mail preferences; and to activate Flashsessions.
	Click to open the Print dialog box, where you can select from the standard print options.
	Click to access the Personal Filing Cabinet, where you can store e-mail messages, Newsgroup messages, and other files.
	Click to set AOL preferences, check personalized stock portfolios, read news and current events, set parental controls, passwords, and Buddy lists.
	Click this button to create links or shortcuts to your favorite Web sites or AOL areas.
	Click to connect to the Web, Internet directories, and Newsgroups.
	Click to access AOL's 21 channels, AOL areas, and Web site connections.
	Click to access the AOL Community Center, Chat Rooms, and meet the stars in the Live chat forum.
	Click to move to keywords or information entered on the URL line.
	Each AOL area has a keyword. Enter the keyword for immediate access to the desired AOL area.

Change Font Size

■ AOL allows you to change font size of your screen text.

    1. Click My AOL button .

    2. Click <u>P</u>references.

    3. Click the General button .

    4. Select a size option.

    5. Click OK .

    6. Close the Preferences dialog box by clicking the Close button (X) in the upper-right corner.

AOL Help

■ AOL offers extensive Help so that you can learn to use AOL effectively.

■ To access Help, click <u>H</u>elp and the help topic of choice from the menu.

Exit AOL

    • To exit AOL, click the close window button ☒ in the upper-right corner of the AOL screen.

    OR

    Click <u>S</u>ign Off, <u>S</u>ign Off on the menu bar.

    OR

    Click <u>F</u>ile, E<u>x</u>it.

America Online: 14

◆ Access the Internet from AOL
◆ Open a Wold Wide Web Site
◆ The AOL Browser Screen
◆ Stop a Load or Search

Access the Internet from AOL

- Click the Internet button on the AOL main screen.

  OR

  Press Ctrl+K, type the word *internet* in the Keyword box and press Enter.

  ✔ *The Internet Connection window displays.*

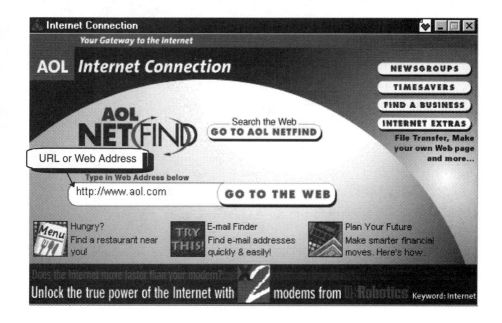

Open a World Wide Web Site

- If you know the Web address (URL), type it into the Type in Web Address below box and click the GO TO THE WEB button `GO TO THE WEB` or press Enter. If the Web address is correct, you will be connected to the Web site.

- If you wish to search the Internet, click the GO TO AOL NETFIND button `GO TO AOL NETFIND`.

The AOL Browser Screen

- Once you are connected to the Web, the screen below displays.

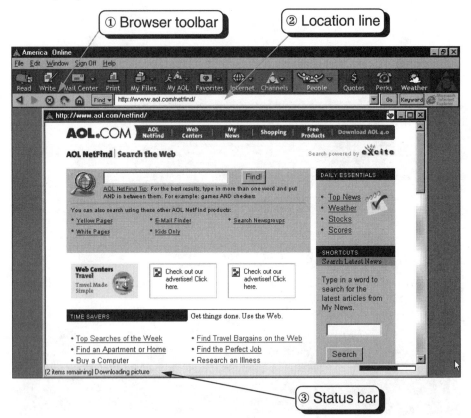

① **Browser toolbar**

- The AOL Browser toolbar will help you navigate through sites you visit on the Web. Buttons on the Browser toolbar also connect you to search and Internet preference areas.

◁	Moves back through pages previously displayed.
▷	Moves forwards through pages previously displayed.
↻	Reloads an image that has been downloaded or restarts a load that has been interrupted. Since the image is stored in the computer's memory, it reloads much faster.
⊗	Stops the loading of a Web page.
⌂	Returns to your home page.
Find ▼	Go here to search the AOL directory using keywords or phrases, to search the Internet, or to find AOL access numbers.

② **Location line**

- AOL stores each Web address you visit during each AOL session. If you wish to return to an address you have visited during the current session, you can click the location box arrow and click the address from the drop-down list.

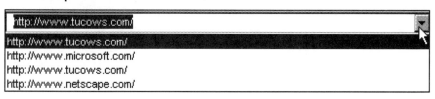

③ Status bar

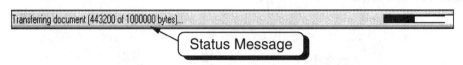

Transferring document (443200 of 1000000 bytes)...

Status Message

- The Status bar, located at the bottom of the screen, is a helpful indicator of the progress of the loading of a Web page. For example, if you are loading a Web site, you will see the byte size of the page, the percentage of the task completed, and the number of graphics and links yet to load. In many cases the time it will take to load the page will display.

Stop a Load or Search

- Searching for information or loading a Web page can be time consuming, especially if the Web page has many graphic images, if a large number of people are trying to access the site at the same time, or if your modem and computer operate at slower speeds. If data is taking a long time to load, you may wish to stop a search or the loading of a page or large file.

  - To stop a search or load click the Stop button on the Navigation toolbar.

  - If you decide to continue the load after clicking the Stop button ![stop], click the Reload button ![reload].

America Online: 15

◆ Favorite Places ◆ Add Favorite Places
◆ View Favorite Places
◆ Delete Favorite Places ◆ AOL History List
◆ Save Web Pages ◆ Print Web Pages

Favorite Places

- A Favorite Place listing is a bookmark that you create containing the title, URL, and direct link to a Web page or AOL area that you may want to revisit.

- The AOL Favorite Place feature allows you to maintain a record of Web sites in your Favorite Places file so that you can return to them easily.

Add Favorite Places

- There are several ways to mark an AOL area or Web site and save it as a Favorite Place. Once the page is displayed:

  1. Click the Favorite Place icon 💙 on the Web site or AOL area title bar.

Favorite Place icon

  2. Click on one of three options that display:

     Add to Favorites

  ✔ *The site will automatically be added to your Favorite Places list.*

  OR

     Insert in Instant Message

✔ *The site will automatically generate an Instant Message screen with a link to the site inserted.*

OR

> Insert in Mail

✔ *The site will automatically generate an e-mail composition screen with a link to the site inserted. Complete this as you would any e-mail message.*

OR

Display the Web page to add, right-click anywhere on the page and select Add to Favorites from the shortcut menu.

View Favorite Places

■ You can view the Favorite Places file by clicking

the Favorites button Favorites on the AOL toolbar and selecting Favorite Places. Click on any listing from the list to go directly to that page.

■ The details of any Favorite Place listing can be viewed or modified by using the buttons on the Favorite Places screen.

Delete Favorite Places

■ You may wish to delete a Favorite Place if a Web site no longer exists or an AOL area no longer interests you.

To delete a Favorite Place:

1. Click the Favorite Places button Favorites on the toolbar.

2. Click Favorite Places.

3. Click on the listing to delete.

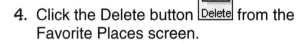

4. Click the Delete button Delete from the Favorite Places screen.

OR

Right-click on the listing and select Delete from the pop-up menu.

OR

Press the Delete key.

5. Click [Yes] to confirm the deletion.

AOL History List

- While you move back and forth within a Web site, AOL automatically records each page location. The History is only temporary and is deleted when you sign off. AOL areas are not recorded in the History list.

- To view the History list, click on the arrow at the end of the URL line. You can use History to jump back or forward to recently viewed pages by clicking on the page from the list.

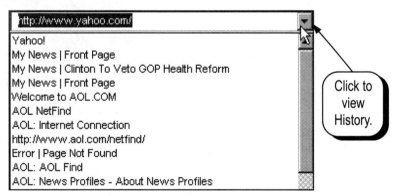

Click to view History.

Save Web Pages

- When you find a Web page with information that you would like to keep for future reference or to review later offline, you can save it.

To save a Web page:

1. Click File, Save.

2. Type a filename in the File name box.

   ✔ *When you save a Web page, often the current page name appears in the File name box. You can use this name or type a new one.*

3. Choose the drive and folder in which to store the file from the Save in drop-down list.

4. Click Save.

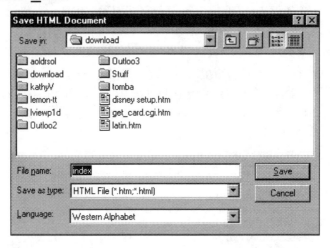

- In most cases when you choose to save a Web page, AOL will automatically save it as an HTML file. Saving a page as an HTML file saves the original formatting and, when accessed, will display as you saw it on the Web.

- You can also save a Web page as a plain text file, which saves only the page text without the formatting or images and placeholders. You might want to do this when saving a very large file, such as a literary work or multiple-page article. To save in plain text format, click the Save as type down arrow in the Save As dialog box and select plain text from the list.

- You can view a saved Web page by clicking File, Open. In the Open a file dialog box, choose the location from the Look in drop-down list and double-click the file name.

Print Web Pages

- One of the many uses of the Internet is to find and print information.

To print a Web page, display it and do the following:

1. Click the Print button on the AOL toolbar.

   OR

   Click Print on the File menu.

2. In the Print dialog box that displays, select the desired print options and click OK.

- In most cases, the Web page will be printed in the format shown in the Web page display.

America Online E-mail: 16

◆ Read New Mail ◆ Compose a New Mail Message
◆ Send Messages ◆ Reply to Mail
◆ Forward Mail ◆ AOL Mail Help

Read New Mail

- There are several ways to know whether you have new mail in your mailbox. If your computer has a sound card and speakers, you will hear "You've Got Mail" when you successfully connect to AOL. The link is replaced by the You Have Mail link, and the mailbox button on the main screen has the flag in the up position .

To display and read new and unread mail:

1. Click the You Have Mail button [You Have Mail] on the AOL main screen.

   OR

   Click the Read button [Read] on the main screen toolbar.

   OR

   Press Ctrl+R.

   ✔ *The New Mail list displays new and unread mail for the screen name used for this session. If you have more than one screen name, you must sign on under each name to retrieve new mail. Click Sign Off, Switch Screen Names to switch names without logging off AOL.*

✔ *New and Unread e-mail messages remain on the AOL mail server for approximately 27 days before being deleted by AOL. If you want to save a message to your hard disk, click File, Save As and choose a location for the message. By default the message will be saved to the Download folder.*

✔ *You can set up AOL to save read messages up to seven days by clicking the My AOL button from the toolbar. Click Preferences, and then click the Mail button* 📧 *. Set the number of desired days in the Keep My Old Mail Online option box.*

2. To read a message, double-click on it from the New Mail list.

Compose a New Mail Message

1. Click Mail Center, Write Mail.

   OR

   Click the Write button Write on the main screen toolbar.

   OR

   Press Ctrl+M.

   ✔ *The Compose Mail screen displays.*

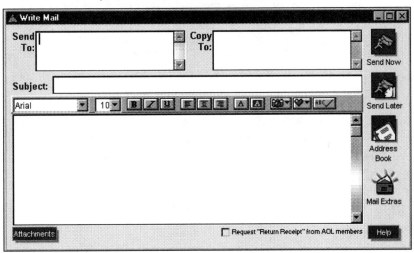

2. Fill in the e-mail address(es) in the Send To box of the Compose Mail screen.

   OR

   Click the Address Book button on the right side of the Write Mail screen and double-click on an entry from your Address Book to insert an address automatically in the address field. (See on page 95 for more information on your Address Book.)

   ◆ If you are sending the same message to multiple recipients, fill in the Copy To (Carbon Copy) box with the e-mail addresses of recipients who will receive a copy of this message. These names will display to all recipients of the message.

   ✔ *Multiple addresses must be separated with a comma.*

   ◆ If you want to send a Blind Copy—copies of a message sent to others but whose names are not visible to the main or other recipients, enclose the address in parenthesis, for example: (joes@ddcpub.com) or click the Blind Copy button

   when inserting addresses from the Address Book.

   ✔ *You can enclose multiple Blind Copy addresses in one set of parentheses, e.g., (joes@ddcpub.com, Zacz).*

3. Fill in the Subject box with a one-line summary of your message. Although AOL will now deliver mail without a heading it's always a good idea to include one. This is the first thing the recipient sees in the list of new mail when your message is delivered.

4. Fill in the body of the message.

Send Messages

- Click the Send button 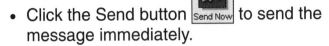 to send the message immediately.

  ✔ *You must be online.*

  OR

  Click the Send Later button 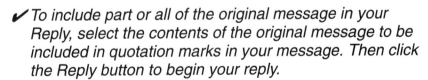 to send a message later that you have composed offline.

Reply to Mail

- You can reply to mail messages while online or compose replies to e-mail offline to send later.

  ### To reply to e-mail:

  1. Click the Reply button ![Reply] from the displayed message screen. If the message has been sent to more than one person, you can send your response to each recipient of

     the message by clicking the Reply to All button ![Reply All] . The addresses of the sender and, if desired, all recipients will be automatically inserted into the address fields.

     ✔ *To include part or all of the original message in your Reply, select the contents of the original message to be included in quotation marks in your message. Then click the Reply button to begin your reply.*

     ✔ *You can select mail preferences like the quotation style by clicking My AOL, Preferences, and the Mail icon.*

2. Click the Send button ![Send Now] if you are online and want to send the reply immediately or click the

Send Later button ![Send Later].

Forward Mail

- There are times when you may want to send mail you receive to someone else.

To forward e-mail:

1. Click the Forward button ![Forward] from the displayed message screen and fill in the address(es) of the recipients of the forwarded message. The Subject heading from the original message is automatically inserted into the subject heading box.

2. Click the Send button ![Send Now] if you are online and want to send the reply immediately or click the Send Later

   button ![Send Later].

AOL Mail Help

- For answers to many of your basic e-mail questions, click Mail Center, Mail Center, and click on the Help button ![HELP] on the Mail Center screen.

America Online E-mail: 17

◆ Add Entries to the Address Book
◆ Enter an Address Using the Address Book
◆ Delete an Address Book Entry

Add Entries to the Address Book

■ Once you start sending e-mail, you may be surprised at how many people you begin to communicate with online. An easy way to keep track of e-mail addresses is to enter them into the Address Book. Once an e-mail address entry has been created, you can automatically insert it into the address fields.

To create Address Book entries:

1. Click Mail Center, Address Book.

   ✔ *The Address Book dialog box displays.*

2. Click the New Person button from the Address Book screen.

   ✔ *The New Person dialog box displays.*

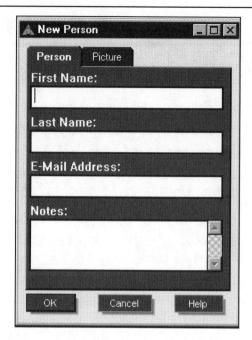

3. Enter the first and last name or a nickname (e.g., JohnV). The name(s) you enter in these boxes is how the entry will appear in the Address Book list.

4. Press the Tab key to move to the E-Mail Address box and enter the complete e-mail address of the recipient.

✔ *When entering the address of an AOL member, you do not need to enter the @aol.com domain information. Enter only their screen name as the e-mail address. For all other Address Book entries you must enter the entire address.*

5. Include any information you might want to remember about the person in the Notes box.

6. Click OK .

Enter an Address Using the Address Book

1. Place the cursor in the address field.

2. Click the Address Book button to open the Address Book.

3. Double-click the name or names from the Address Book list to insert in the Send To or Copy To address box using the appropriate buttons from the Address Book screen.

✔ *Unlike addresses entered in the Send To or Copy To address fields, addresses entered using the Blind Copy feature will not be visible to other recipients of the e-mail message. Clicking the Blind Copy button* after *selecting an address from the Address Book inserts the address in the Copy To box in parentheses.*

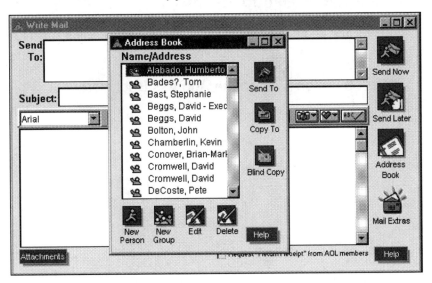

4. Click ☒ in the upper right-hand corner to close the Address Book.

To add an Address Book entry from mail received:

1. Open the e-mail message.

2. Click the Add Address button  from the message screen.

3. Enter the first and last name of the sender. The information entered into these fields will appear in the Address Book listing.

   ✔ *Notice that the e-mail address has been filled in for you.*

4. Enter any information you may want to remember about the person in the Notes box.

5. Click OK .

To create a Group Entry:

1. To enter a Group listing (e.g., Book Club), click the New Group button on the Address Book screen.

2. Enter the Group Name.

3. Enter the full e-mail addresses of each person in the group. Press Enter after typing each address.

4. Click [OK] when done.

Delete an Address Book entry

1. Click Mail Center, Address Book to open the Address Book.

2. Select the name to delete.

3. Click the Delete button [Delete].

4. Click Yes to confirm the deletion.

5. Click [X] in the upper right-hand corner to close the Address Book.

America Online E-mail: 18

◆ Add Attachments to a Message
◆ Open an E-Mail Attachment

Add Attachments to a Message

■ Any type of file can be sent as an attachment to an e-mail message—including text files, graphics, spreadsheets, and HTML documents.

To attach files to a message:

1. Compose the message to be sent. (See **Compose New Message** on page 91.)

2. Click the Attachments button [Attachments] at the bottom of the Write Mail screen.

3. Click the Attach button [Attach].

4. Select the drive and folder where the file you wish to attach is located.

5. Double-click the file to attach from the Attach File dialog box.

✔ *Multiple files can be sent by repeating the steps above. After you have selected the multiple attachments that will accompany the e-mail message, AOL will automatically combine these files into one compressed file called a zip file. If the recipient is not using AOL 4, he or she will need a file decompression program such as PKZIP or WINZIP to open the file.*

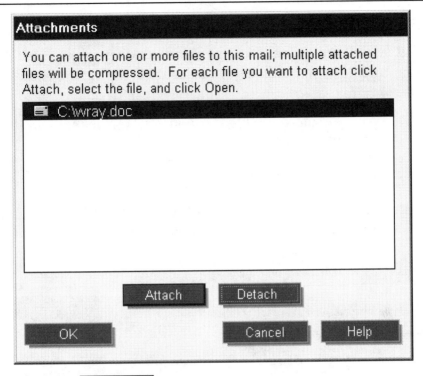

6. Click [OK].

✔ *The attachment will appear at the bottom of the Write Mail screen next to the Attachments button.*

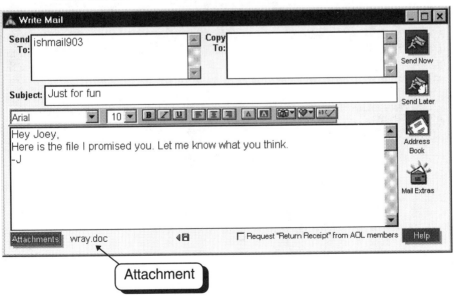

Attachment

7. If you are online, click the Send button 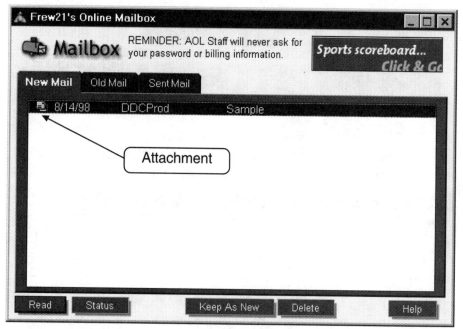Send Now to send the message immediately, or click the Send Later button

Send Later to store the message in your Outgoing Mail if you are working offline.

Open an E-mail Attachment

- An e-mail message that arrives with a file attachment is displayed in your new mail list with a small diskette icon under the message icon.

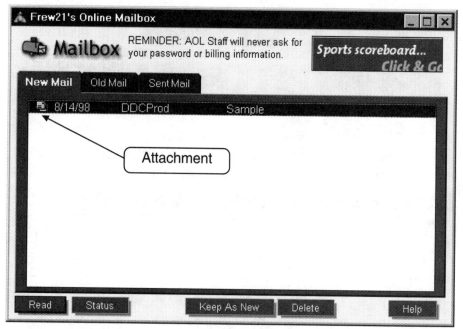

- Opening the message and viewing the attachment are two separate steps:

  1. Open the message by double-clicking on it from the New Mail list. The message will display.

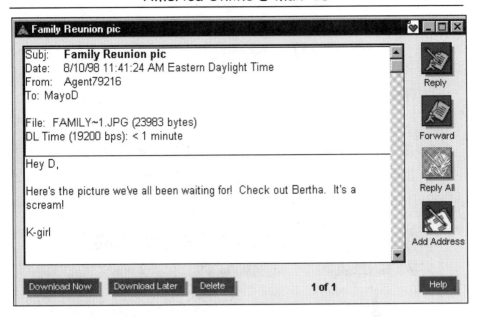

2. You can choose to download the file attachment immediately by clicking the Download Now button Download Now at the bottom of the displayed message screen. Click the Save button Save on the Download Manager screen to save the file, by default, to the AOL4.0/Download folder. If you desire, you can change the save destination folder (see page 104).

✔ *A status box will display while the attachment is being downloaded or transferred to your computer.*

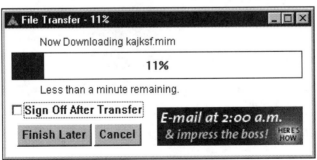

✔ *Click the Sign Off After Transfer checkbox if you want AOL to disconnect automatically when the transfer is complete.*

3. At the end of the download, the file transfer box will close and you will get a message confirming that the file has been transferred. Click OK .

OR

You may choose to download the file later. Click the Download Later button Download Later to store the message in the Download Manager. When you are ready to download the file, click My Files, Download Manager, and then select the file to download. You must be online.

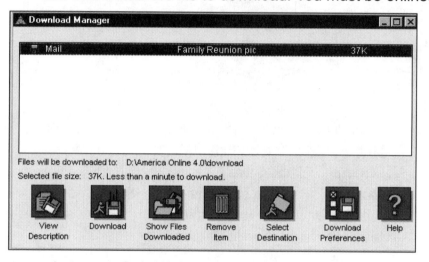

To change the default location of where files are stored:

1. Click the My Files button from the AOL toolbar.

2. Click Download Manager and then the Select Destination button from the Download Manager screen.

3. Select the desired destination from the Select Path dialog box.

✔ *All files will be automatically downloaded to this location.*

Search Engines: 19

◆ Surfing vs. Searching ◆ Search Sites
◆ Search Basics

Surfing vs. Searching

■ The Web has many thousands of locations, containing millions of pages of information. Unfortunately, the Internet has no uniform way of tracking and indexing everything.

■ Initially, it may seem easy to do research on the Web— you just connect to a relevant site and then start clicking on links to related sites. This random method of finding information on the Internet is called *surfing*. It may be interesting and fun, but there are drawbacks. Surfing is time consuming and the results are frequently inconsistent and incomplete. It can also be expensive if you are charged fees for connect time to your Internet Service Provider.

■ *Searching* is a more systematic and organized way of looking for information. You can connect to one of several search sites that use *search engines* to track, catalog, and index information on the Internet.

Search Sites

■ A *search site* builds its catalog using a search engine. A search engine is a software program that goes out on the Web, seeks Web sites, and catalogs them, usually by downloading their home pages.

■ Search sites are classified by the way they use search engines to gather Web site data. On the following page is an explanation of how the major search services assemble and index information.

Search Engines

- Search engines are sometimes called *spiders* or *crawlers* because they crawl the Web.

- Search engines constantly visit sites on the Web to create catalogs of Web pages and keep them up to date.

- Major search engines include: AltaVista, HotBot, and Open Text.

Directories

- Search *directories* are created by people who catalog information by building hierarchical indexes. Directories may be better organized than search engine sites, but may not be as complete or up-to-date as search engines that constantly check for new material on the Internet.

- Yahoo!, the oldest search service on the World Wide Web, is the best example of an Internet search directory. Other major search directories are: Infoseek, Magellan, and Lycos.

Multi-Threaded Search Engines

- Another type of search engine, called a *multi-threaded* search engine, searches other Web search sites and gathers the results of these searches for your use.

- Because they search the catalogs of other search sites, multi-threaded search sites do not maintain their own catalogs. These search sites provide more search options than subject-and-keyword search sites, and they typically return more specific information with further precision. However, multi-threaded search sites are much slower to return search results than subject-and-keyword search sites.

- Multi-threaded search sites include SavvySearch and Internet Sleuth.

■ If you are using Internet Explorer or Netscape Navigator, you can click on the Search button on the toolbar to access a number of search services.

Search Basics

■ When you connect to a search site, the home page has a text box for typing the words you want to use in your search. These words are called a *text string*. The text string may be a single word or phrase.

■ Once you have entered a text string, initiate the search by either pressing the Enter key or by clicking on the search button. This button may be called Search, Go Get It, Seek Now, Find, or something similar.

■ For the best search results:

- Always check for misspelled words and typing errors.

- Use descriptive words and phrases.

- Use synonyms and variations of words.

- Find and follow the instructions that the search site suggests for constructing a good search.

- Eliminate unnecessary words (the, a, an, etc.) from the search string. Concentrate on key words and phrases.

- Test your search string on several different search sites. Search results from different sites can vary greatly.

- Explore some of the sites that appear on your initial search and locate terms that would help you refine your search string.

Search Engines: 20

◆ Simple Searches ◆ Refine a Search ◆ Get Help

Simple Searches

- Searches can be simple or complex, depending on how you design the search string in the text box.

- A *simple search* uses a text string to search for matches in a search engine's catalog. A simple search is the broadest kind of search.

  - The text string may be specific, such as *Social Security*, *current stock quotes*, or *Macintosh computers*, or it may be general, such as *software*, *economy*, or *computer*.

  - The catalog search will return a list, typically quite large, of Web pages and URLs whose descriptions contain the text string you want to find. Frequently these searches will yield results with completely unrelated items.

- When you start a search, the Web site searches its catalog for occurrences of your text string. The results of the search are displayed in the window of your browser.

- Each search site has its own criteria for rating the matches of a catalog search and setting the order in which they are displayed.

- The catalog usually searches for matches of the text string in the URLs of Web sites. It also searches for key words, phrases, and meta-tags (key words that are part of the Web page, but are not displayed in a browser) in the cataloged Web pages.

- The information displayed on the results page will vary, depending on the search site and the search and display options you select. The most likely matches for your text string appear first in the results list, followed by other likely matches on successive pages.

✔ *There may be thousands of matches that contain your text string. The matches are displayed a page at a time. You can view the next page by clicking on the "next page" link provided at the bottom of each search results page.*

■ You can scan the displayed results to see if a site contains the information you want. Site names are clickable links. After visiting a site, you can return to the search site by clicking the Back button on your browser. You can then choose a different site to visit or perform another search.

Refine a Search

■ Suppose that you only want to view links that deal with Greek tragedies. Note, in the example below, the number of documents that were found when *Greek tragedies* was entered in this search. Since the search string didn't include a special *operator* to tell the search engine to look for sites that contain both Greek *and* tragedies, the results display sites that contain Greek *or* tragedies in addition to sites that contain Greek *and* tragedies.

Number of documents

Search [the Web ▼] for documents in [any language ▼]

Greek tragedies

search *refine*

Help . Preferences . New Search . Advanced Search

Click to find related books at **Amazon.com.**

About **269396** documents match your query.

1. **Ruth Hazel, Greek Tragedies in Modern British Theatres**
   To "Crossing the Stages" Home Page. Crossing the Stages: The Production, Performance and Reception of Ancient Theater. Ruth Hazel Department of Classical..
   http://www.usask.ca/classics/abstracts/hazel.html - size 3K - 28-Sep-97 - English - *Translate*

■ To reduce the number of documents in this search, use operators—words or symbols that modify the text string instead of being part of it. Enter *Greek,* space once, then enter a plus sign (+) and the word *tragedies* (Greek +tragedies) then click Search. This tells AltaVista to look for articles that contain Greek *and* tragedies in the documents. Note the results that display when the plus is added to the search.

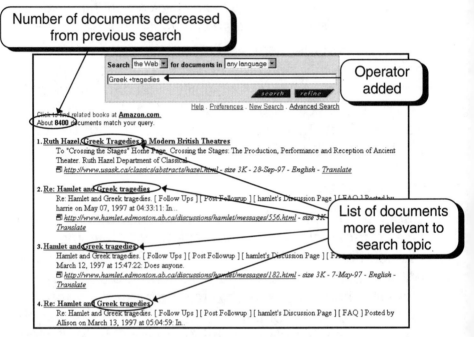

- The number of results is dramatically reduced, and the documents displayed display information that is more closely related to the topic, *Greek tragedies*.

- You can also *exclude* words by using the minus sign (-) to refine a search further and eliminate unwanted documents in the results. For example, if you wanted to find articles about Greek tragedies but not ones that deal with Hamlet, enter a search string like this: *Greek +tragedies -Hamlet*. Note the different results that display in the following example:

Alta Vista Web Pages (1-20 of 6255)

- Grene, David: The Complete **Greek Tragedies**: Sophocles I - Grene, David, editor/translator The Complete **Greek Tragedies**: Sophocles I. [I]Oedipus the King[I],[I]Oedipus at Colonus[I],and [I]Antigone[I]. With an...
  --http://www.press.uchicago.edu/cgi-bin/hfs.cgi/00/7374.ctl

- Grene, David: The Complete **Greek Tragedies**: Euripides V - Grene, David and Richmond Lattimore, editors The Complete **Greek Tragedies**: Euripides V. [I]Electra[I]. Translated and with an Introduction by Emily...
  --http://www.press.uchicago.edu/cgi-bin/hfs.cgi/00/862.ctl

- Grene, David: **Greek Tragedies** - Grene, David and Richmond Lattimore, editors **Greek Tr**...
  three paperback volumes. Volume I. Edited by David Grene and Richmond...
  --http://www.press.uchicago.edu/cgi-bin/hfs.cgi/00/7699.ctl

- Grene, David: The Complete **Greek Tragedies**: Sophocles II - Grene, David and Richmond Lattimore, editors The Complete **Greek Tragedies**: Sophocles II. [I]Ajax[I]. Translated and with an Introduction by John Moore....
  --http://www.press.uchicago.edu/cgi-bin/hfs.cgi/00/864.ctl

- Grene, David: The Complete **Greek Tragedies**: Euripides I - Grene, David and Richmond Lattimore, editors The Complete **Greek Tragedies**: Euripides I. With an Introduction by Richmond Lattimore. [I]Alcestis[I]....
  --http://www.press.uchicago.edu/cgi-bin/hfs.cgi/00/858.ctl

- Grene, David: The Complete **Greek Tragedies**: Euripides II - Grene, David and Richmond Lattimore, editors The Complete **Greek Tragedies**: Euripides II. [I]The Cyclops[I] and [I]Heracles[I]. Translated and with...
  --http://www.press.uchicago.edu/cgi-bin/hfs.cgi/00/859.ctl

- Aeschylus II (The Complete **Greek Tragedies**) - Text-Only. Aeschylus II (The Complete **Greek Tragedies**) by David Grene, Richmond Lattimor (Editor) List: $8.95 Our Price: $8.95. Availability: This item...

No reference to Hamlet in any of the documents

Get Help

- Check the Help features on the search tool that you are using to see what operators are available. Since there are no standards governing the use of operators, search sites can develop their own.

Search Engines: 21

◆ AltaVista ◆ Yahoo! ◆ excite

- Web searches can be frustrating. There are, however, a few basic tips that will almost always help you find what you want.

- Following are search tips for three of the most popular search sites. Each search site is different but some search techniques are universal.

AltaVista

http://altavista.digital.com/

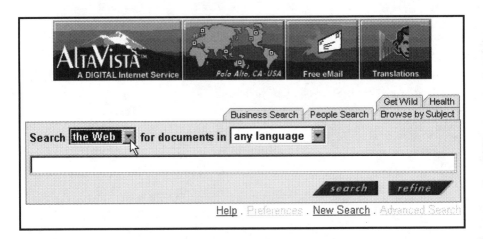

- Enter your text string in the Search box. Make sure all words are spelled correctly.

- You may modify your search string with operators to narrow the search results. This will help you find more information specifically relevant to your search.

  - To modify your search string, put a (+) in front of the words that *must* be in your results and a (−) in front of the words that must *not* be in your results.

- Always use lowercase letters when searching the Web using AltaVista unless you are using proper nouns.

- You can also enter exact phrases into the search text box. If you are looking for pages that contain an exact phrase, enclose the phrase in the Search box with quotation marks.

- Search Usenets (Newsgroups) to read public opinion and postings on thousands of topics.

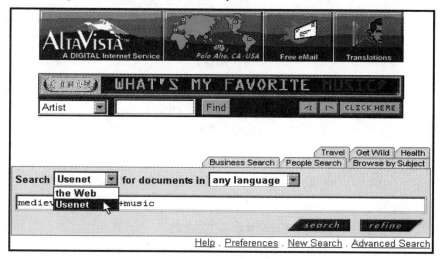

- Go to the AltaVista search areas found at the top of the search box to search a collection of Web pages and sites on everything from Travel to People.

- Click on AltaVista *Help* to get more information on searches.

Yahoo!

http://www.Yahoo.com

- Yahoo! searches for information in the four databases contained in its search catalog:

  - **Yahoo! Categories:**
    Web pages organized under different categories such as History, Economy, and Entertainment.

  - **Yahoo! Web Sites:**
    A list of Web page links that are relevant to your search.

  - **Yahoo!'s Net Events & Chat:**
    A list of events and live chats on the Web that are relevant based on words in your search string.

  - **Most Recent News Articles:**
    A database of over 300 online publications for articles that contain your keywords.

- Enter the keywords of your search in the search box. Make sure the words are spelled correctly.

- Be as specific as possible when entering keywords into the search box.

- Use a **(+)** in front of any keyword that must appear in the document and a **(-)** in front of words that should not.

- Yahoo! provides search syntax options to help you modify your search.

- To display search syntax options, click the *options* link next to the Search button from the home page. The following dialog box displays:

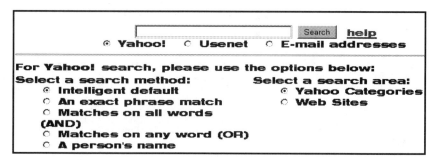

- You can also do a search by document title and URL.

- Place a *t:* in front of one or more keywords to yield Web pages with the keywords in the title of the page.

- Place a *u:* in front of keywords to yield returns with the keyword in the URL. Your search should return pages dedicated to the subject of your keywords.

- Yahoo! has specialized search areas. Click on any of the links on the Yahoo! home page to search for anything from stock quote information to buying a pet or an automobile. These links contain extensive information.

excite

http://www.excite.com/

- excite searches the Web by concept using Intelligent Concept Extraction (ICE) to find the relationships between words and ideas.

- Enter concepts and ideas rather than keywords into the search box.
- You can further modify your search by adding words supplied by excite based on the keywords or phrase you've entered.

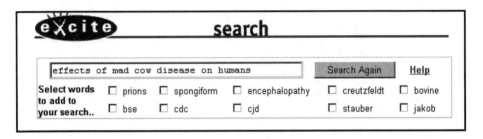

- Modify the words in your search phrase by using the (+) and (−) signs.
- Click *Help* to read more on excite search.
- You can activate a Power Search. This search uses the excite Search Wizard to help focus your search.
- Click the *Power Search* link located to the left of the search box on the excite home page. Enter the keywords or idea into the search box, as shown below.

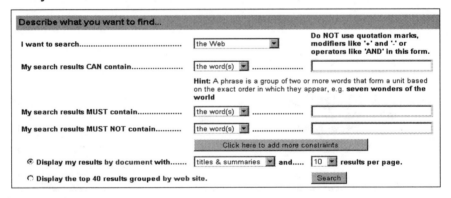

- Leisure-Time Pleasures
- Travel Sites
- All in the Family
- Just for Seniors
- Money Matters
- Read All About It
- Computer Troubleshooting
- Support

WEB RESOURCES

What's Cooking?

◆ Epicurious ◆ The Food Network's CyberKitchen
◆ Baker Boulanger ◆ Other Sites

If the smell of spaghetti sauce simmering on the stove or a cake baking in the oven makes your mouth water, be sure to see what's cooking on the Web. With hundreds of food sites you can find recipes for everything from gourmet French cuisine to eating-light menus.

Epicurious

http://food.epicurious.com/

 With over 10,000 recipes from *Gourmet* and *Bon Appétit* magazines, this site is for the passionate cook.

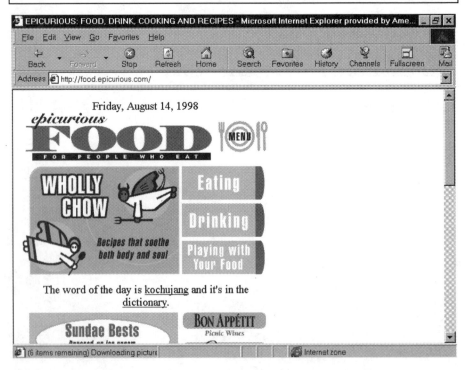

- From the home page click on *Wholly Chow* to locate recipes for when you are feeling naughty or nice. The recipes here are divided into two categories. Select from either the *Cooking for Health* or *Forbidden Pleasures* recipe drop-down lists:

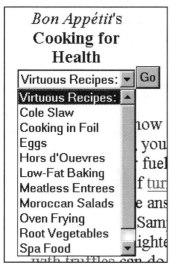

- Select a category, click *Go* and then choose from an abundance of either fitfully-good or decadently-delicious recipes.

- Click the *Recipes* link on the home page to search the Epicurious database. The recipe file can be searched by keyword, cuisine, course, main ingredient, or by an extensive list of preparation options:

Preparation	⊙ May include any selection ○ Must include all selections	
⊓ Advance	⊓ Lowfat	⊓ Sauté
⊓ Bake	⊓ Marinade	⊓ Smoke
⊓ Grill	⊓ Microwave	⊓ Steam
⊓ Broil	⊓ Poach	⊓ Stew
⊓ Fry	⊓ Quick	⊓ Stir-Fry
⊓ Light	⊓ Roast	

- Epicurious also includes wine suggestions, restaurants of note, and useful cooking tips.

The Food Network's CyberKitchen
http://www.foodtv.com/

 Now when you want to find a new recipe you no longer need to flip through your crusty, old cookbooks. Watch the chefs in action on The Food Network, then print out the recipes from their online site.

- If recipes are what you're after, click *Recipes* on the top of the home page. The Food Network breaks the recipes down by television show. Illustrated below is a sample of their listings:

Hot Off the Grill with Bobby Flay	Tamales World Tour	Too Hot Tamales
The Essence of Emeril	Emeril Live	Cooking Monday to Friday
Taste	Chef Du Jour	Molto Mario
Specials	Cooking Live	Dining Around
Pasta Monday to Friday	Michael's Place	Gourmet Getaways with Robin Leach
Bakers' Dozen	Pick of the Day	Bill Boggs Corner Table
Grillin' and Chillin'	Two Fat Ladies	Mediterranean Mario

- Click on a link to access the recipes from recent shows. You can also find out when the program regularly airs and what some of the upcoming recipes will be, so you can watch the chef as she or he executes the recipe.

- Other features of this site include a question and answer forum with their CyberChef, a CyberMarket (where you can purchase, among other things, cookbooks by the featured chefs), a bimonthly wine article, and restaurant reviews.

Baker Boulanger

http://www.betterbaking.com/

Some people say "I love you" with a fresh batch of chocolate chip cookies or the ultimate birthday cake. If you fall into this category—or you just enjoy baking—be sure to explore this baking site.

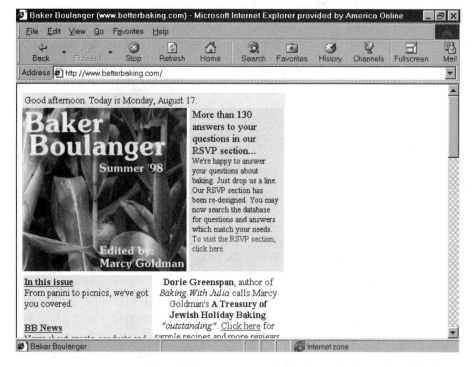

- This site satisfies both sweet and savory cravings with hundreds of recipes for cakes, cookies, eclairs, breads, biscuits, and more.

- From the home page, click on the *Recipes* link. Select *Feature archives* to search by recipe names or *Category listing* to search on such categories as scones, bagels, bread, biscotti, etc.

- In addition to the baking recipes, Baker Boulanger also throws in some excellent meat, fish, and poultry recipes to fill in the gaps before desert.

- Be sure to click the *In this Issue* link on the home page to read featured articles and recipes.

Other Sites

Betty Crocker
http://www.bettycrocker.com/

♦ The weekly menu planner, which includes dinner recipes for an entire week, is one of the many practical and delicious features of this site. You can also pick out recipes from the site and then print out a custom-made shopping list.

Better Homes and Gardens Kitchen
http://www.bhglive.com/survival/

♦ From an established name in domestic wisdom, this site features hundreds of recipes. Also see **How Does Your Garden Grow** on page 127.

The Internet Chef On-Line Magazine
http://www.ichef.com/

♦ Browse through hundreds of recipes at this eclectic site.

Gourmet Goodies Online

◆ Virtual Vineyards ◆ Fancy Foods Gourmet Club
◆ Other Sites

If you feel life's many pleasures can be summed up by the words "food and drink," then you'll be in for some tasty treats at these great gourmet sites. The offerings in this section will please the most discriminating palates. If you love to cook or want a prepared feast delivered to your door, these sites will show you how to get gourmet goodies online.

Virtual Vineyards

http://www.virtualvin.com/

Wine is the operative word at this site. Choose from hundreds of wines from many small but important vineyards in a wide range of categories and prices.

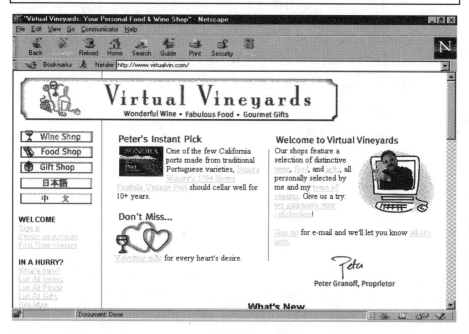

- From the novice to the connoisseur, Virtual Vineyards has something for everyone. They offer delicious wines from small vineyards and provide a comprehensive description of each featured vineyard and their wines. In every case, you have a real sense of what you're buying.
- The site frequently offers specials on selected wines. Discounted wines tend to move quickly and the selections change often, so check the site often.
- You need a major credit card to set up an account. Most items are shipped within two days of receipt of the order. Check the site for shipping options.

Fancy Foods Gourmet Club
http://www.ffgc.com/

 This site is not for the casual cook. The information found here is dedicated to visitors who have a certain taste for the art of cooking and fine food.

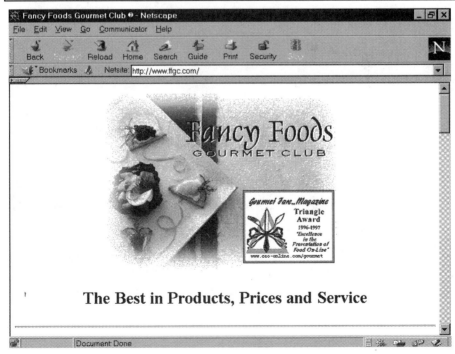

- The Fancy Foods Gourmet Club online catalog is filled with pages of fine foods for the discriminating palate. The Fancy Foods catalog is distinguished not only by numerous awards for their food products, but also by their quality, limited availability, and great prices.

- All items are 20-50% below average gourmet shop prices. Shop this site for the best in caviar, cheeses, chocolates, pâtés, and desserts. However, don't get too carried away: expensive shipping fees for perishable food can really add up.

- Full gourmet meals are also available for purchase. The menus range from scones and gourmet jellies for breakfast in bed to hearty seafood dinner extravaganzas that include smoked Coho salmon, duck liver mousse, and raspberry linzer tortes.

- The quality of all the items offered by the Fancy Foods Gourmet Club is guaranteed. You can order online with a Visa or MasterCard.

Other Sites

Digitalchef

http://www.digitalchef.com/

+ This site is a joint effort with the Culinary Institute of America. Visit this site for a one-stop supplier of gourmet foods and cookware.

Wine Navigator

http://homearts.com/helpers/winenav/wine.htm

+ The Wine Navigator can help you choose the right wine for the right price. There are links to a glossary of terms, tips on buying and storing wine, and advice on how to match wine with food.

How Does Your Garden Grow?

◆ Better Homes and Gardens: Gardening Home Page
◆ GardenNet ◆ The Rose Resource ◆ Other Sites

If gardening is one of your favorite pastimes, be sure to explore all that's blooming on the Internet. Order gardening supplies and seeds, read advice from gardening experts, and share your enthusiasm with other green thumbs.

Better Homes and Gardens: Gardening Home Page

http://www.bhglive.com/gardening/

From a leading name in gardening, see what's growing on the Gardening home page.

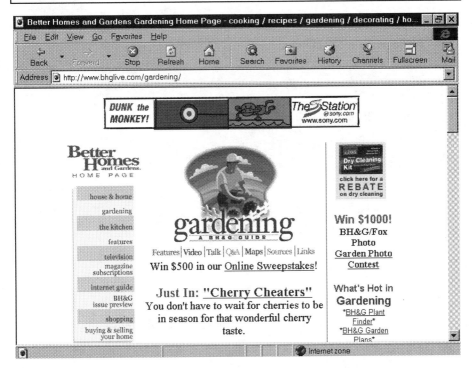

- *Better Home and Gardens'* site is pleasing on many levels—not only are the pages budding with information, but the material is presented in a clear and easy-to-follow manner.

- If you are about to plant a garden or do any kind of landscaping, spend some time with the Editor's Choice Plant Finder. This feature is a catalog of trees, shrubs, and flowers and how they fare in different climates, so you can find the best plants for your own backyard.

- And, after you have had your fill of all that's green and flowery, be sure to explore *Better Homes and Gardens'* other pages.

GardenNet

http://www.gardennet.com/

 Organized by topics—such as *how-to & equipment, garden design*, and *garden services*—this site is loaded with information.

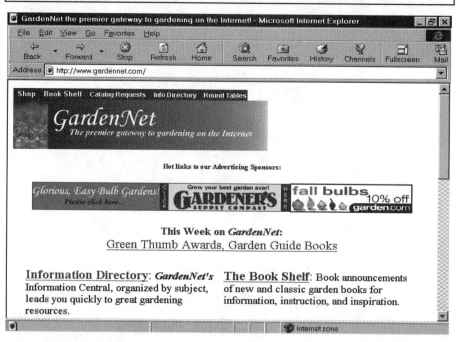

- The GardenNet's Guide to Gardens of the USA is a lovely feature of this site. Using GardenNet's extensive catalog of US gardens, search by state or garden type. For each listing, there is a brief description of the garden, garden hours, how long it takes to walk through the gardens, and, if available, a link to the garden's Web page. To access the garden database, click the *Guide to Gardens of the USA* link on the home page.

- If you don't want to wait for catalog delivery, explore GardenNet's links to online gardening shopping.

The Rose Resource

http://www.rose.org/

 This site is wonderful for the rose enthusiast—from the experienced to the aspiring rose gardener, as well as anyone else who enjoys the beauty of the rose.

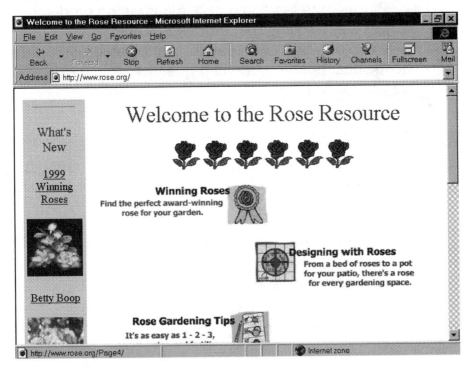

- This site, brought to you by All-America Rose Selections, is thoroughly committed to roses. Though Gertrude Stein did say, "a rose is a rose is a rose . . .," the AARS proves that the world of roses—with hundreds of varieties—is enormous.

- With rose growing tips, suggestions on designing with roses and arranging roses, photos of award winning roses, and a helpful tip of the month, this site is a must-see for rose lovers.

- And for those who really have been bitten by the rose bug, this site even goes into the history of roses, dating back to the first fossil record, believed to be 3.5 billion years ago.

Other Sites

Burpee Web Site

http://garden.burpee.com/

+ Burpee, the leading name in gardening products, has been selling garden seeds since 1876. Visit the site to get a free catalog, place an order, read recipes, post a gardening question, and more.

Gardenscape Ltd.: Fine Garden Tools & Accessories

http://www.gardenscape.on.ca/

+ Order all your garden supplies, products, and gifts at this site.

Garden Solutions

http://www.gardensolutions.com/cgi-bin/WebObjects/GardenSolutions

+ In addition to gardening supplies that you can order from this site, Garden Solutions posts a helpful gardening tip every day.

Fun and Games

♦ 19thHole.com ♦ Yahoo! Games ♦ CryptoPlus
♦ Other Sites

Using the Internet for research is unbeatable, but don't forget to explore the lighter side of what's out there. There are sites devoted to every kind of recreational activity.

19thHole.com

http://19thhole.com/

 For millions of Americans, golf is synonymous with leisure. If it's raining out and you can't make it to the course, spend some time golfing on the Internet.

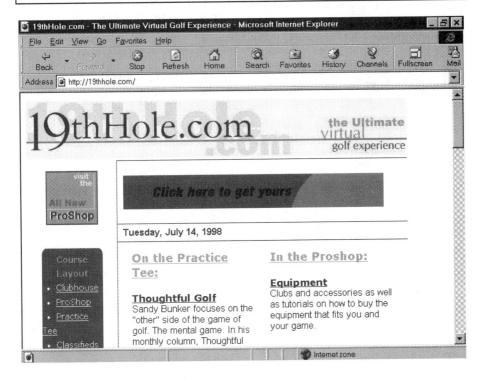

- Voted best of the Web 1998 by SelectSurf, Best of the Web 1997 by Snap!, and NetGuide Gold Site 1997, this site has articles, merchandise, golf pointers, and more. 19thhole.com is every golf lover's dream.
- Click on *The Best on the Net* to access an enormous database of additional golf sites and listings.

There are now 714 sites in the database.

- **Accessories** (51)
- **Art** (11)
- **Classifieds** (4)
- **College** (15)
- **Course Design/Mgmt** (1)
- **Courses** (121)
- **Entertainment** (2)
- **Equipment Makers** (17)
- **Fantasy Leagues** (4)
- **Games** (3)
- **General** (49)

- **News** (6)
- **Organizations** (15)
- **Other Golf Stuff**
- **Personal Sites** (2)
- **Players** (17)
- **Pro Shops** (6)
- **Publications** (30)
- **Regional** (1)
- **Software** (0)
- **Sports** (4)
- **Talk** (3)
- **Tournaments** (32)
- **Travel** (41)

Yahoo! Games

http://play.yahoo.com/games

There are several great things about this site: you play the games with real people not against a software program, there is no software to download and all the games are free. Just register, sign on, and begin playing.

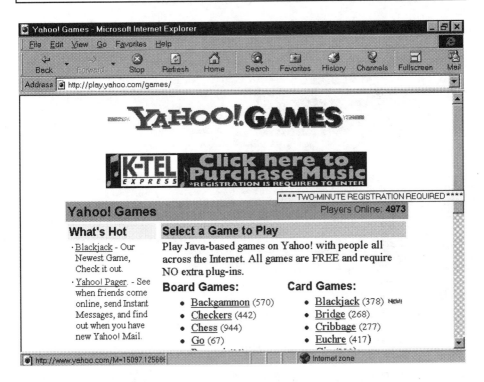

■ These games are best played using Netscape or Explorer. When you visit the site for the first time you have to register by choosing a unique Yahoo! Games ID and password. After your ID is accepted, you can begin to play. You will receive a confirmation of your ID by e-mail.

- To play such games as blackjack, checkers, chess, bridge, cribbage, hearts, and gin, simply click on the desired link from the Yahoo! Games page. The games take about a minute to load, and then you can start.

- From each game page, click on the *Cases Ladder* link to play tournament style against other players. You report your wins and losses to the Case Ladder service to keep track of how you rank with other players.

- Once you enter the desired game area, click on one of the area links from social to advanced.

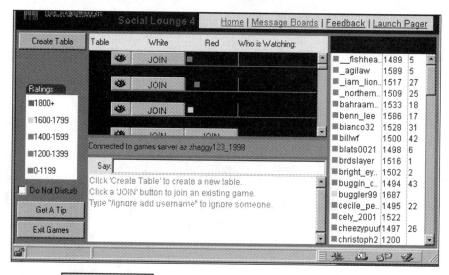

- Click [Create Table] to start a new table and wait for players, or click [JOIN] to participate in an existing game. The [image] allows you to watch a game being played.

- From the specific game area click the *Rules* link to get information on how to play the particular game or click the *Yahoo! Category* link to see links to relevant sites on the Web.

- You can also participate in live chats with other members in the game area.

CryptoPlus

http://www.cryptoplus.com/

 If you are a cryptogram lover and word puzzle aficionado, CryptoPlus is for you. This site features daily cryptograms, downloadable word games, and more.

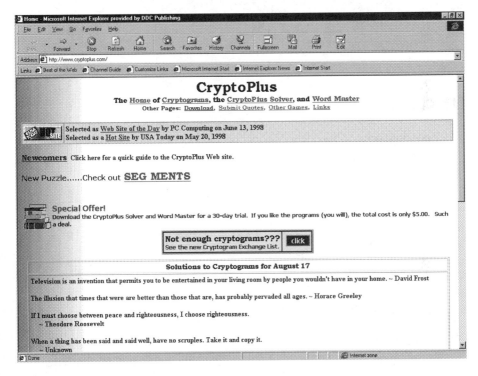

- With accolades from *USA Today* and *PC Computing*, CryptoPlus bills itself as *the* cryptogram site on the Web. If you're visiting this site for the first time, click the *newcomers* link on the home page for a guide to this site's features.

- This site is updated daily with four new cryptograms. Cryptograms are words or phrases written in a code that you need to break. Quotation categories include celebrity, literary, historical, and wildcard. Solutions are posted the following day.

- Be sure to try the CryptoPlus Solver—a program that lets you toss out the paper and pencil and solve puzzles in a flash. It's free to download and try for 30 days and $5.00 to keep.

- You can also download other logic games, submit quotes, meet fellow cryptogram fans in the cryptogram exchange program, and create your own cryptograms to send to your friends.

Other Sites

Jeopardy Online

http://www.station.sony.com/jeopardy/

- Take the Jeopardy challenge, play Wheel of Fortune, and other game shows—all online. You must first register with the Sony Station to begin playing the games.

Gamesville™

http://www.bingozone.com/

- Go to this site to play Bingo! The game is open from 10 am–4:00 am EST. Win cash prizes and, the best part—you don't have to pay to play. The advertisers pay all costs. You must register before you play.

Arts & Crafts

◆ Michaels®: The Arts and Crafts Store™
◆ I-Craft ◆ Other Sites

Though in many ways the computer age seems antithetical to handicraft skills, you can find a wealth of online arts and crafts sites. Explore project ideas, suppliers, sewing and knitting patterns, and much more.

Michaels®: The Arts and Crafts Store™

http://www.michaels.com/

 The name Michaels®—an arts and crafts superstore—is synonymous with handicrafts.

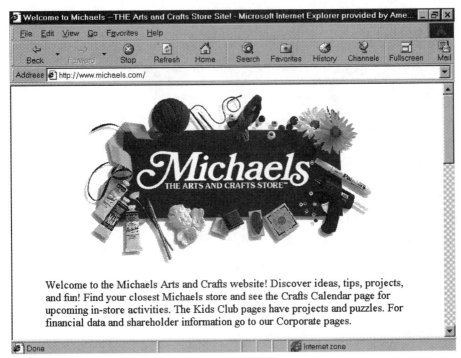

Welcome to the Michaels Arts and Crafts website! Discover ideas, tips, projects, and fun! Find your closest Michaels store and see the Crafts Calendar page for upcoming in-store activities. The Kids Club pages have projects and puzzles. For financial data and shareholder information go to our Corporate pages.

- Click on the *Projects* link on the home page to begin browsing the extensive project archive. New projects are listed on the top of the page, followed by recently archived Michaels' projects. If you have a project in mind but can't locate it in the recent catalog of projects, click *Search* at the bottom of the page to check the archives.

- When the grandkids or your favorite young neighbor is visiting, click on the *Kids' Club Projects* from the Projects page for dozens of kid-friendly activities. When you have decided which project to make, click the *Locate* link on the home page to find the nearest Michaels store, where you can purchase all the needed supplies.

I-Craft

http://www.i-craft.com/

 Sponsored by the Hobby Industry Association, founded in 1940, this site promotes crafts as "one of the world's most rewarding pastimes."

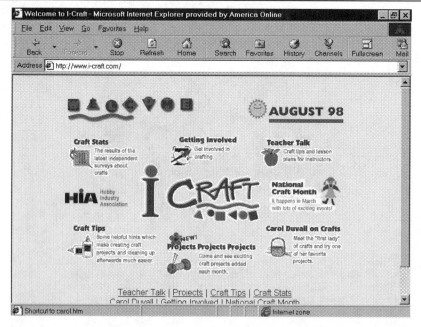

■ With new projects added monthly, this site is sure to provide you with lots of wonderful projects. Click on *Projects, Projects, Projects* to begin. Illustrated below is a sampling of the types of activities that you can find at this site.

- **Memory Album** [NEW]
  Perfect for saving those summer vacation memories

- **3D On A Curve** [NEW]
  Unique and colorful decorative hatbox

- **Safari Wall Hanging**
  Fun project for a hot summer day

- **Gold Memory Album**
  Create a stunning hand bound memory album that will become a family treasure

- **Cut & Decorated T-Shirt**
  For that casual summer party!

- **Etching A Monogram Illuminated Letters**
  Etch your initials and create an heirloom monogram

■ If you are going to be spending any quality time with a youngster, click on *Teacher Talk* for creative project ideas that combine history, holiday, and nature with crafts.

■ From *Carol Duvall on Crafts*, star of a *Home and Gardens* channel's TV show, try one of Carol's favorite projects.

Other Sites

Aleene's

http://www.aleenes.com/

- This site's motto—"changing lives through creativity"—sums up what you will find here. Join Aleene's Creative Living Online Project Library for hundreds of crafts projects.

Knitting

http://knitting.miningco.com/

- This knitting page is just a list of links to lots of knitting sites. Links to information on knitting stitches, free patterns, chat rooms, and more.

Mining Co. Crafts for Kids

http://craftsforkids.miningco.com/

- With everything from "silly recipes" to "paper-plate animals," this site provides loads of activities for when you'll be spending time with a youngster.

www.quiltersweb.com

http://www.quiltersweb.com/

- A must-see for quilters, this site offers books, fabrics, and tools you can purchase online. Get online quilting lessons and download free patterns. Also view an extensive online gallery.

Cheap Seats (Airfare)

◆ TWA Senior Travel Pak
◆ Continental Airlines: Seniors Programs
◆ ltravel.com ◆ Other Sites

If you're looking for the cheapest airfares around, search the many bargain fares that are available to older flyers. Also try online discount travel sites. As an added bonus, you can often make hotel and car rental arrangements at these sites.

TWA Senior Travel Pak

http://www.twa.com/schedules/sr_senior_travel.html

TWA's Senior Travel Pak is a great way to go. If you are 62 or older, TWA's travel coupons are a deal.

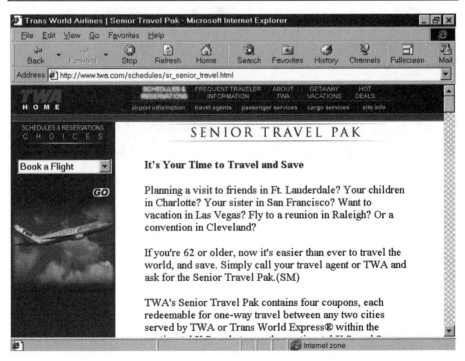

- TWA Senior Travel Pak is simple and straightforward. At the time of this book's publication, the cost was $548 per Pak of four tickets—that's just $137 a flight.

- The Pak includes four one-way flight coupons that can be used for travel to any TWA destination in the US, or between the US and San Juan, Montego Bay, Santo Domingo, and Toronto, Canada. For the frequent flyer, coupon books with eight one-way tickets are also available. The cost is $1032.00—just $129 per flight.

- TWA also offers discount senior fares to Europe. Check the site for additional information and restrictions.

Continental Airlines - Seniors Programs

http://www.flycontinental.com/products/senior/

Continental Airlines offers books of tickets as well as other services and discounts for people 62 and older.

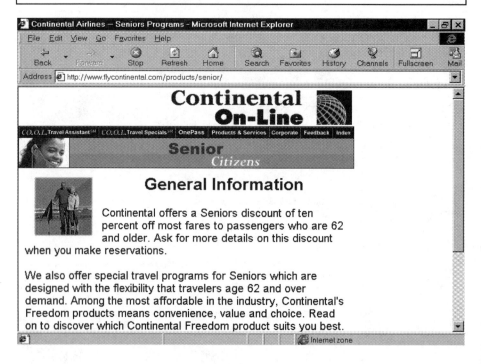

- Continental has two discount packages for flyers 62 or older: The Freedom Trips and Freedom Passport. The Freedom Trips are flight coupons (four for $579 or eight for $1,079) that can be used for one-way travel in the US, Canada, Mexico, and the Caribbean. The Freedom Passport is an amazing deal for the frequent traveler: It is good for unlimited foreign or domestic travel and can be purchased for four or twelve month periods. Be sure to check the ground rules to see if this program is right for you.

- In addition to the package plans, Continental offers travelers 62 and older 10% discounts on most flights. Check the Continental Seniors page for details and restrictions.

1travel.com

http://1travel.com/Welcome.htm

Use 1travel's interactive database of fares and flight information to find bargains. You can also check airline regulations and your rights as a passenger.

- 1travel.com is a ticket consolidator. Ticket consolidators buy tickets in bulk to hundreds of destinations from many different airlines so they can offer deeply discounted fares directly to the public.

- Here you can find discounts on one-way fares, business class, and first class fares to select destinations.

- Click the Travel Guide link on the home page for general information on your destination including weather, vital statistics, tourism contacts, foreign exchange rates, health services, accommodations, and holidays and events.

- 1travel.com also has a unique link called *Rules of the Air*. This link answers questions you may have concerning check-in times and carry-on baggage limits by airline. It also outlines your rights as a passenger if, for example, your flight is overbooked or what your options are if your flight is delayed.

Other Sites

FareFinder

http://www.reservations.com/Farefinder/

- To find the lowest airfares available, check Preview Travel's FareFinder service. Enter your departure and destination cities to find the lowest fares currently available.

Hilton Senior HHonors

http://www.hilton.com/^hhonors2/seniors/ index.html

- Save 20%-50% on room rates and 20% off on dinner for two at over 400 hotels worldwide. Go to the site for details and restrictions.

Travel Adventures

◆ Elderhostel ◆ ElderTreks
◆ Golden Escapes: Tours for the 50-plus Traveler
◆ Other Sites

Being senior does not have to mean being sedentary. Many senior-specific excursions are designed to be challenging to the body as well as the mind.

Elderhostel

http://www.elderhostel.org/

With a motto of "adventures in lifelong learning," Elderhostels are for the curious traveler who likes to explore new places and learn new things.

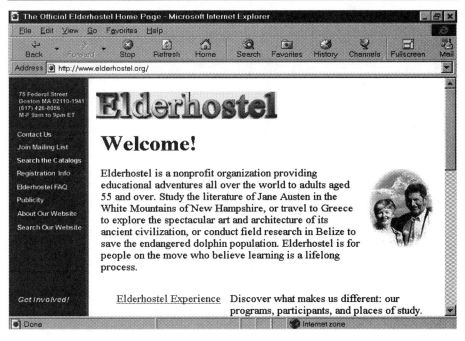

- Elderhostel is a nonprofit organization that organizes educational vacations—most of which last a week. If you are new to ElderHostels, click on *First Time Visitors* to find out the basics, including FAQs (frequently asked questions), eligibility information, and available special-needs services.

- Click *About Our Catalogs* to search the online database of programs or to order a printed catalog.

- The average tuition for a week-long program is around $400 (transportation not included). Eldershostel also offers Hostelships, which are financial grants for programs. Click on *Scholarship* on the Elderhostel Experience page for qualification information.

ElderTreks

http://www.eldertreks.com/

Don't let the nondescript home page of this site fool you: ElderTrek trips are anything but ordinary!

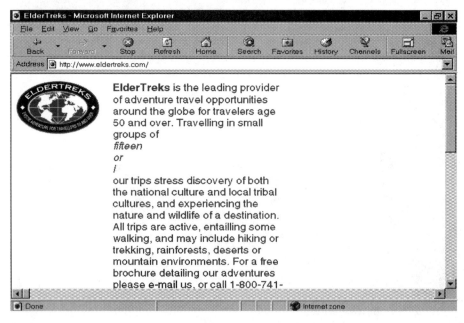

ElderTreks is the leading provider of adventure travel opportunities around the globe for travelers age 50 and over. Travelling in small groups of
fifteen
or
l
our trips stress discovery of both the national culture and local tribal cultures, and experiencing the nature and wildlife of a destination. All trips are active, entailling some walking, and may include hiking or trekking, rainforests, deserts or mountain environments. For a free brochure detailing our adventures please e-mail us, or call 1-800-741-

- ElderTrek trips are designed for travelers aged 50 and older who want to go beyond the conventional sightseeing package. The traveler becomes completely submerged in the culture, rather than simply observing it. This is *not* sightseeing through a tour bus window.

- Click on *Scheduled Departures* to see a list of upcoming trips. Each tour is rated by degree of physical activity.

SOUTH EAST ASIA	
Thailand	◑◑
Laos	◑◑
Vietnam	◑◑
Borneo	◑◑◑
HIMALAYAS	
Yunnan	◑◑◑
Tibet	◑◑◑◑
Nepal	◑◑◑
Bhutan	◑◑◑
INDONESIA	
Sumatra	◑◑
Java/Bali	◑◑
Irian Jaya	◑◑◑◑

Guide to the Physical Activity Rating: In order to assist you in determining which trip is appropriate for you, we have assigned each tour an "Activity Rating". The rating is a blend between the overall activity rating of a tour and infrastructure demands such as roads and accommodations. The more physically demanding a trip, the higher the rating.

- The above sample of the ElderTrek locations gives an idea of some of the exotic destinations. Keep in mind, the more physically demanding trips are not for everyone.

Golden Escapes: Tours for the 50 plus Traveler
http://www.goldenescapes.com/

This company, in operation since 1977, arranges group tours for senior travelers.

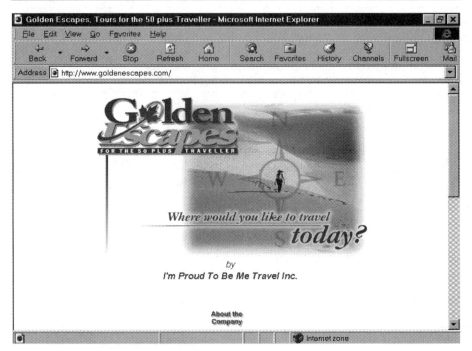

- There are several ways to find trips at this site. First, click *The Tours* link on the home page. Then you can search by *Country* from a drop-down menu. Or, you can search seasonal listings broken down into the following categories: *North American Holidays*, *British, European & Mediterranean Holidays*, and *Exotic Adventures & Unique Holidays*.

- Golden Escape's trips are not geared towards the frugal traveler; they are aimed at adventurers who enjoy a little bit of luxury. Trips range from long weekends to several weeks.

Other Sites

ThirdAge Marketplace - The Cruise Center

http://www.thirdage.com/market/renaissance/

- The ThirdAge site (see **Resources Galore**) has joined efforts with Renaissance cruises to organize trips for ThirdAgers.

Grand Circle Travel Online

http://www.gct.com/

- Visit this site to learn about "unique experiences for seasoned travelers" ages 50 and older.

QTW-Senior Travel

http://www.quinwell.com/senior.html

- Come to this site for discount travel tours for those 50 and older.

Family Trees

◆ Genealogy—AT&T WorldNet® Service
◆ The USGenWeb Project
◆ Genealogy Gateway ◆ Other Sites

Though it may seem ironic to trace the past using the latest technology, the Internet is quickly becoming the preferred tool of genealogists.

Genealogy—AT&T WorldNet® Service

http://www.att.net/find/genealogy/

 The AT&T site maintains a well-selected assortment of resources for the beginner as well as the experienced genealogist.

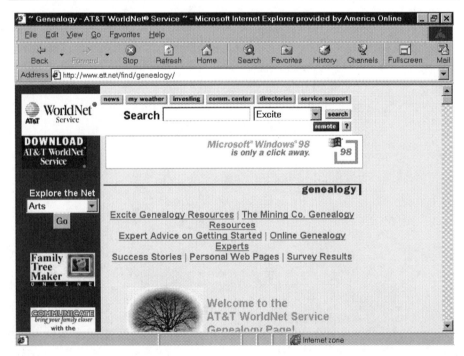

■ A good place to start is by clicking on the *Mining, Co.* link. The Mining Co. always provides top quality resources. The Mining Co. organizes its information by main category. Click on a category and then choose from a list of articles. The *Genealogy 101* link, for example, provides nearly a dozen interesting articles. (See the **Grandparenting** topic for another great Mining Co. collection.)

■ From the AT&T home page, click on *Helm's Genealogy Toolbox* for an enormous guide to genealogical sites. The Helms, a husband and wife team who are expert online genealogists, contribute their resources and their knowledge of the field in a comprehensive getting started area. Click on *Expert Advice* to access this information.

The USGenWeb Project

http://www.usgenweb.org/

This non-profit site run by volunteers is dedicated to providing online genealogists information about the ancestry of every county and state.

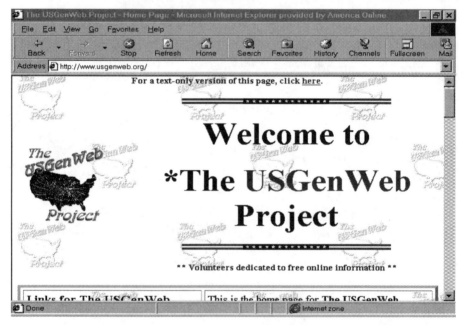

- The USGenWeb site is a great place to start if you are new to genealogy. Click the *Information for Researchers* link on the home page for all the basics—including vocabulary, tips on locating immigration records, hints for finding maiden names, and the *Helpful Hints for Beginning Researchers* link that opens the door to even more "how-to" information.

- If you already know the tricks of the trade and you wish to search a particular state, click either the *Map* or *Table* link on the USGenWeb home page. Then click on a state or state name to begin your survey. The information available for each state varies.

- Because volunteers run this site, the people involved with these pages are always happy when new genealogy enthusiasts want to get involved. Click on the *Information for Current and Prospective Volunteers* link for information.

Genealogy Gateway

http://www.gengateway.com/

The Genealogy Gateway is the largest source of genealogical information, with over 46,000 listings and free services.

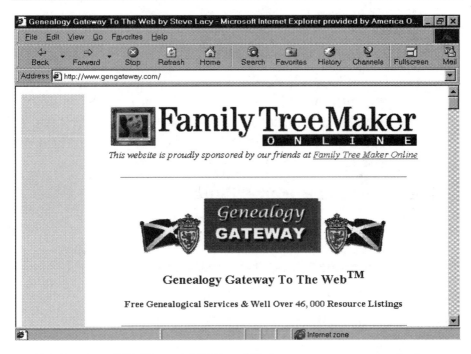

- While the AT&T and USGenWeb pages are good places to find basic information about getting started, you can go to the Genealogy Gateway pages when you know what you wish to find. Though the resources here are enormous, this site does not provide much introductory, getting-your-feet-wet material.

- What this site *does* provide for the seasoned genealogist is incomparable to other Internet resources. Search on surnames, military service (mostly Civil War records), obituaries, marriage records, as well as government databases and extensive information on Scotland and Ireland.

- Click on the *Family Tree Maker Online* link on the top of the home page to search a 153-million name database and to register to receive genealogical newsletters. Also, find out about Family Tree Maker, a genealogical software program.

Other Sites

RootsWeb

http://www.rootsweb.com/

- This site's mission is to provide the genealogical community with information and support, including access to Newsgroups and Mailing Lists. (See **Newsgroups** and **Mailing Lists** for information on how to participate in these groups.)

The Genealogy Home Page

http://www.genhomepage.com/

- Be sure to bookmark this site and return to it frequently to see the constantly updated genealogical resources.

Genealogy Links & Information

http://ravenwing.com/genealogy/links.html

- Just as the name implies, this page is a catalog of links. This site maintains an extensive collection of Native American genealogical links.

Grandparenting

◆ The Foundation For Grandparenting
◆ Grandparenting—Senior Living ◆ Other Sites

Though the concept of being a grandparent has been around for ever, the term *grandparenting* is relatively new. Grandparenting is all about grandparents—or anyone of an older generation—interacting with the younger people in their lives. Many active grandparents are taking their thoughts and experiences to the Web.

The Foundation For Grandparenting

http://www.grandparenting.org/

 The Foundation For Grandparenting supports "Grandparent Power" by promoting the important—but too often undervalued—role that grandparents play.

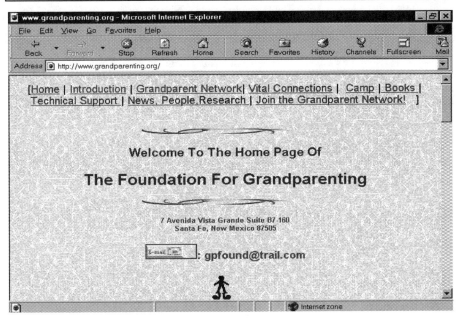

- Click on the *Camp* link on the top of the home page to learn about a wonderful summer experience that you can have with your grandchild. The week-long summer activities include nature hikes, storytelling, square dancing, cookouts, and much more.

- For a tax-deductible donation of $20, you can receive *Vital Connections*, the organization's quarterly publication that features articles, news, and views on grandparenting.

Grandparenting—Senior Living

http://seniorliving.miningco.com/msub8.htm

If you want the ultimate guide to grandparenting sites, be sure to visit this site, one of the Mining Co.'s interest areas.

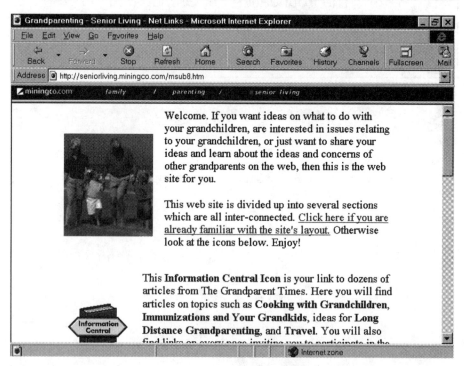

- The Mining Co., which has compiled this page, has a unique approach to finding information on the Web. The Mining Co. catalog is broken down into over 500 special interest topics. Each section is led by "Guides." The Guide points you to links of interest, and you can also search the site by interest areas, subsections, or related ideas. The catalog is constantly monitored and updated.

- Featured links may be to topics such as the ones listed below.

> Ask CGA
> Feature Articles
> In Granpa's Words
> Kitchen Korner
> Long-Distance Grandparenting
> One Step Ahead
> Let's Keep Them Safe and Sound
> Sharing the Caring
> The Travel Times
> Triple Talk: Practical Tips for Three Generations
> **NEW**◆Cartoons

- From the Grandparenting page, be sure to click the *Senior Living* link for wonderful resources on senior health, wealth, wisdom, and more.

Other Sites

Grandtravel

http://www.grandtrvl.com/

- Founded on the belief that grandparents and grandchildren make wonderful travel companions, Grandtravel offers worldwide travel opportunities designed for multigenerational travel teams. Come to the site for full details on all the available trips.

Net Pet Care

◆ The Pet Channel ◆ Healthy Pets ◆ Other Sites

The positive effect our four-legged friends have on our daily lives is absolutely invaluable. If for no other reason, we owe it to our pets to learn how to care for them properly. Get online advice on the most effective ways to care for your pet from nutritional information to preventative health care to fun training techniques.

The Pet Channel

http://www.thepetchannel.com/index.html

This comprehensive site for pet lovers includes topics on pet health, training, products (including a Kitty Safari videotape), and more.

- This site has it all: click on *pet horoscopes* to learn about your pet's astrological makeup or click *PET HEALTH* to learn precautions to take when your pet is out in the heat too long. For both the fun and serious side of caring for your trusty companion, this site contains tons of information.

- If you are interested in adopting a pet, click *FIND A PET*. From here you can search on either *shelters & rescues* or *breeds & breeders*.

- The Pet Channel has established forums for dog lovers, cat people, equestrians, birds of a feather, and for those who love all other types of animals. Click *user forums* from the home page to access these question and answer areas. (See **Newsgroups** on page 201 for basic information on how to work with Newsgroups.)

Healthy Pets

http://www.healthypet.com/

Dogs and cats are the most popular pet choices. As a result, this site is loaded with information on caring for these two animals.

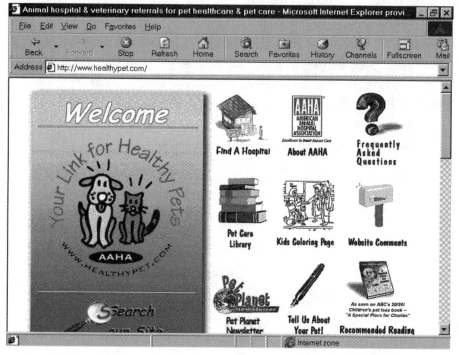

- The American Animal Hospital Association (AAHA) maintains this site, an organization of over 13,000 veterinarians. AAHA asserts that pets are important members of your family, so you should treat them as such. Proper care includes annual physical examinations, vaccinations, dental care, diet, and exercise. The Healthy Pets site deals with all of these topics and more.

- Go to the Pet Care Library for answers to health questions, animal behavior, and the best training methods for your pet. Get training hints for housetraining puppies and kittens, and learn how to prevent bad behavior in dogs and cats.

- Click on *Find A Hospital* to locate an AAHA-accredited veterinary hospital anywhere in the United States or Canada. From the Hospital page you can also access and complete a first-aid chart that has life-saving tips on what to do in a pet emergency.

Other Sites

Purina Pets for People Program

http://sun6.dms.state.fl.us/citytlh/animal/adoption/purina.html

- This program offers pets, free of charge, to qualifying senior citizens 60 years of age or older.

Senior Citizens Best Friends: Pets

http://seniors-site.com/pets/pets.html

- Two seniors created this site in loving memory of their pet. Many of the resources on this site focus on coping with the loss of a pet.

Healthy Paws

http://healthypaws.com/index.html

- At this site you can purchase a variety of things for your animal—from dog sweaters to pearl necklaces for your cat. You can also find facts on pet vitamins as well as general heath.

Delta Society

http://www2.deltasociety.org/deltasociety/

- The Delta Society mission statement is "To promote animals helping people improving their health, independence, and quality of life."

Resources Galore

- ◆ AARP (American Association of Retired Persons)
  - ◆ SeniorCom ◆ ThirdAge
  - ◆ Senior Cyborgs ◆ Other Sites

The online senior community is *the* most quickly growing Internet market. As a result, more and more sites cater to senior surfers' needs and interests. Many long-standing seniors' organizations are taking their content to the Internet. In addition, many new resources are making their debut online.

AARP (American Association of Retired Persons)

http://www.aarp.org/

AARP is a nonprofit organization that strives to help older Americans, "achieve lives of independence, dignity, and purpose."

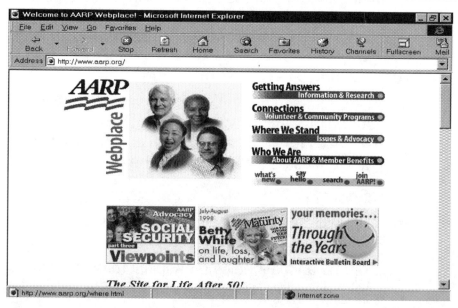

- AARP has been in operation since 1958, and with 33 million members, their presence can't be ignored.

- The benefits of visiting the AARP site are tremendous. Even if the only thing that you do at the site is register to become an AARP member, then your visit was worthwhile. If you are over 50, for eight dollars a year you will receive *Modern Maturity*, AARP's publication, and—here's where membership really pays off—reduced costs on prescriptions, online services, hotels, car rentals, and countless other discounts. You don't need to be retired to join AARP and membership includes spouses.

- The AARP site includes articles on critical topics like investing wisely, reverse mortgages, caregiving, and much more. In addition to the daily articles, you can access AARP's regular features by clicking any of the main links on the home page.

SeniorCom

http://senior.com/

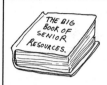

This seniors' site recently won the NetGuide's Platinum award for its excellence. Explore the many resources available at SeniorCom.

- This site got started when Tom Poole, the company President and CEO, tried to find online information about senior living communities. His discovery: very limited information that was difficult to find, at best. Poole started SeniorCom, which is receiving rave reviews as it caters to the fast-growing population of surfing seniors.

- Much of the information at this site addresses major issues and concerns—such as health care, residence alternatives, a directory of practicing doctors in the United States, and information on financial matters.

- From the home page, click on one of the major topics to get started.

SENIORCOM MONEY CLUB

PRIME LIFESTYLES

SENIOR CHAT

SENIOR NEWS NETWORK

TOWN SQUARE

HEALTH AND WELLNESS

PROFESSIONAL SERVICES

TRAVEL

DOCTOR DIRECTORY

- In addition to the above areas, the home page features news articles, special offers, and general interest stories.

- To participate in the Senior Chat, Bulletin Board, or Community Calendar, you must first register. Registration is easy to do and free.

ThirdAge

http://www.thirdage.com/

ThirdAge (thurd'aj): (n.) 1. A time of life characterized by happiness, freedom, and learning. 2. A life stage following "youth" and preceding "old age". 3. A Web site where like-minded people find intelligent conversations and useful tools. 4. Your best years yet!

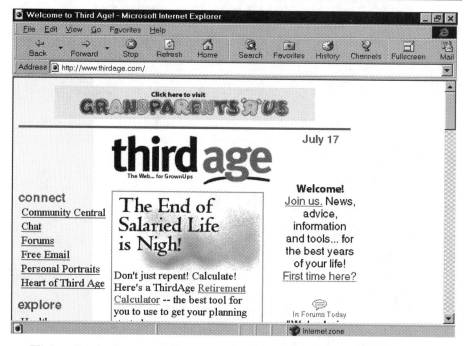

- This site is for you if you consider yourself: self-reliant, involved, experience-seeking, socially aware, or curious.

- Here you will find both practical and extracurricular information, with topics that vary from coping with grandkids to Suzi's Loveseat, ThirdAge's resident sex expert.

- The ThirdAge site is excellent for browsing. Start by selecting a featured topic or click on one of the main categories to begin. (Be sure to check out the *Tech* link for computer forums, news, tools, and general info and resources.)

Senior Cyborgs

http://www.online96.com/seniors/

If you want to go cyber, you might as well go all the way with Senior Cyborgs. Though the home page may look extraterrestrial, you will find that most of the information here is very down to earth.

- This site strives to provide those over 50 and their friends and family (including children, partners, and caregivers) senior-savvy content with a forum for expressing ideas, information, and concerns.

- Senior Cyborgs provides general senior-focused information that you may find at other senior sites in addition to some more progressive topics.

The Senior's File Index

Senior File Homepage || Health & Medicine || Legal Links || Politics & Government || Disabilities || Consumer & Finance || Fun & Leisure || Travel Services || Housing & Retirement || NJ Links || Chat Room || Links || Gay Seniors || Home & Garden || Offers & Promotions || Insurance || Classifieds || Gerontology || Genealogy || Death & Dying || Pets || Meeting Places || Books & News || Shopping || Sponsors & Advertising || Medical Euipment & Supplies || Online96 Mall || Contact Us

- Each main category link reveals an abundance of resources—including excellent links to government services, Newsgroups, Mailing Lists, and related topics.

Other Sites

Seniors-Site.com

http://seniors-site.com/

- ♦ This site is the superstore of all senior sites.

Age of Reason.com

http://www.ageofreason.com/

- ♦ Come to this site to explore over 5,000 links for Internet surfers 50 and older.

Funsites Guide to Web sites for Seniors & Retirement

http://www.funsites.com/ki-seniors.html

- ♦ The Funsites guide includes retirement, shopping, games, and other categories of senior links.

Advocacy and Legislation

◆ The National Council on the Aging
◆ The National Council of Senior Citizens
◆ Other Sites

Seniors' rights in the United States are too often neglected. Know your rights and learn about the many advocate organizations aggressively taking a stand for the rights of older Americans.

The National Council on the Aging

http://www.ncoa.org/

NCOA is a nonprofit organization that takes active interest in improving both public and private policies affecting older persons.

- The NCOA's mission is to safeguard the rights of older Americans. Top stories cover such topics as threats to Medicaid and Medicare, the Older Americans Act, House budgetary concerns, and Social Security.

- The NCOA is one of the founding members of The Leadership Council of Aging Organizations (LCAO), a coalition of nonprofit organizations that focus on the well-being, needs, and rights of older Americans. From this site, you can access the LCAO home page, which offers a wealth of links to diverse resources such as National Senior Citizens Law Center and the Older Women's League.

- Click on the *FAMILY CARE RESOURCES* picture on the bottom of the home page to access an extensive archive that includes tips, tools, and documentation on recent research. Many of the articles provide links to additional sites and most pages contain an e-mail address to contact for additional information.

FAMILY CARE RESOURCES

- While most of the information at this site is free, additional information, benefits, opportunities, and services can be accessed through membership. Membership dues are $75 ($45 if you are a retiree). With membership you receive *NCOA Networks*, a bimonthly news digest, and the quarterly journal, *Innovations in Aging*, which covers critical issues and information for older persons.

- Membership also includes access to NCOA professional networks, called Constituent Units, which include such focus groups as Health Promotion Institute (HPI) and National Institute on Financial Issues and Services for Elders (NIFSE).

The National Council of Senior Citizens

http://www.ncscinc.org/

In the early 1960s, the NCSC started as a healthcare advocacy organization for seniors. Today the NCSC continues to fight for the rights of older Americans.

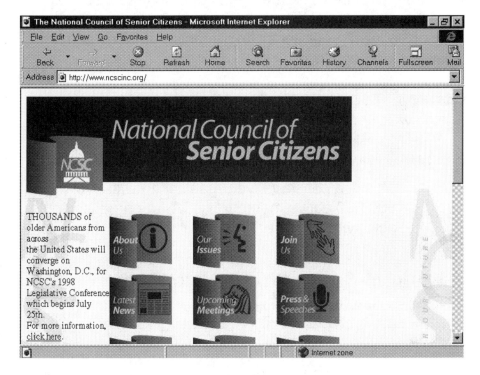

- The NCSC takes an aggressive stance on fighting for the social and financial rights of the elderly. This group is up-front about their activism and is willing to take on government giants in their battle.

- The NCSC has taken on such issues as Medicare, Medicaid, Social Security, managed care, and affordable housing.

- From the home page, click on *Join Us* to become an NCSC member. Members enjoy the bimonthly magazine *Seniority*, which includes articles on governmental issues, health tips, and financial advice; a monthly newsletter; and discount coupons for prescriptions, dental care, vision care, Medicare supplemental insurance, NCSC credit cards, savings programs, and automobile insurance. The cost of membership is only $7 annually.

- Even if you are not a member, you can take advantage of the articles and information that these advocates have to offer. Keep your finger on the pulse of many senior issues and concerns.

Other Sites

United Seniors Association

http://www.unitedseniors.org/

- This is a conservative organization with over 500,000 active members. USA (the organization's acronym) fights for retirement security for all Americans.

National Senior Citizens Law Center

http://www.nsclc.org/

- The NSCLC mission is to assist older Americans to live with dignity, security, and freedom from poverty. The organization maintains a strong legal team to aid and assist the elderly.

NCPSSM

http://www.ncpssm.org/menu.html

- The National Committee to Preserve Social Security and Medicare is an advocacy group—with over 5.5 million members—dedicated to seniors' rights.

Home Is Where the Heart Is

◆ HUD: Senior Citizens ◆ The Retirement Net
◆ Senior Living Alternatives
◆ LivOn Senior Living Online Network
◆ Other Sites

When it is a time for a lifestyle change or you just need information on your rights as a homeowner or renter, check out the resources available to you online.

HUD: Senior Citizens

http://www.hud.gov/senior.html

Part of the HUD (Department of Housing and Urban Development) site, these pages address housing concerns and housing rights for all senior citizens.

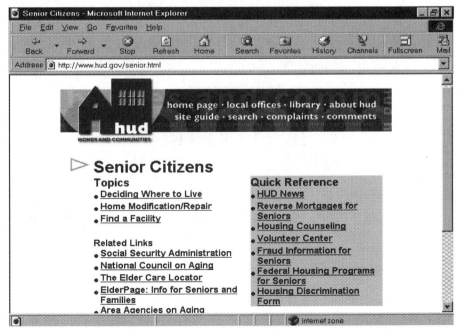

- The HUD site provides solid information for all seniors—regardless of whether you're a home owner or a renter, or you're looking for a luxury retirement community or federally funded housing.

- If you are in a period of transition, click on the *Deciding Where to Live* link on the home page to find out about residential options.

> - **Housing Choices**
> - **Decisions About Retirement Living**
> - **Guide to Choosing a Nursing Home**

- For refinancing information, click on the *Reverse Mortgages for Seniors* link to find out how you can convert the equity of your home into liquid funds.

- The *Volunteer Center* is a wonderful area to explore both federal and community organizations that depend on the generosity of volunteers. Many of the volunteer programs are senior-specific.

> - **Senior Service Corps** (Corporation for National Service)
>   - o **Foster Grandparents**
>   - o **The Senior Companion Program**
>   - o **The Retired and Senior Volunteer Program**

- In addition to the terrific housing links and information, check out other valuable resources under *Related Links*.

The Retirement Net

http://www.retirenet.com/

The Retirement Net caters to seniors who are still active but wish to live in a retirement community.

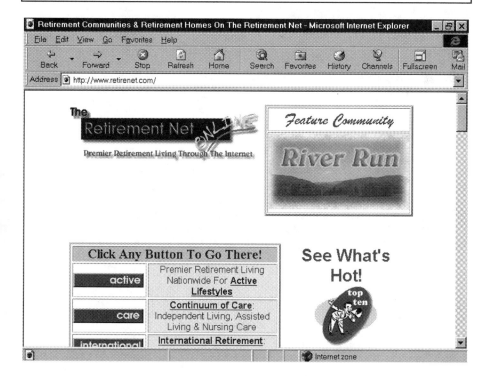

- Though the site does have extensive listings for nursing homes and assisted living, the site's focus is on retirement communities for active seniors.

- International retirement communities organized by country, retirement communities with golf courses, and resort senior living are some of the categories you can explore.

Senior Living Alternatives

http://www.senioralternatives.com/

With terrific listings organized by state, explore the lifestyle options that are available.

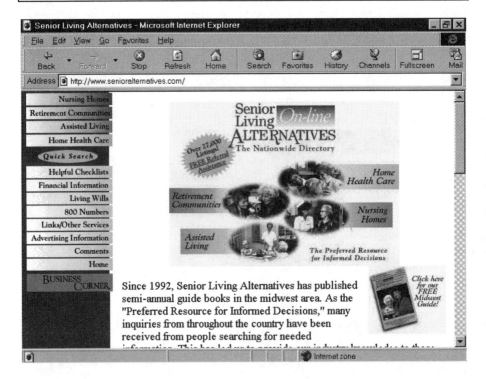

- The first stop that you should make on the Senior Living Alternatives home page is the *Helpful Checklist* link. From the checklist page click on the lifestyle that interests you (retirement, assisted living, home health care, or nursing home). From there, read the basics of your selection, find out what to look for in a provider, and follow a checklist to see if your needs match your lifestyle choice.

- Use the Quick Search feature to search on retirement, assisted living, nursing care, or home health care. Search by city, state, or ZIP code to get a list of residences and services. The comparative shopping feature allows you to view several programs at once so that you can compare features online.
- The site also provides financial and legal information, as well as a selection of excellent senior links.

LivOn Senior Living Online Network

http://www.livon.com/

 LivOn maintains a database of over 60,000 senior housing care facilities—from independent living to nursing home facilities—all over the country.

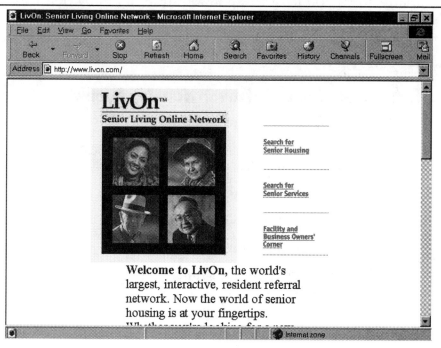

- To begin using this site, click on the *Search for Senior Housing* link on the bottom of the page.

Search for Senior Housing

Search for Senior Services

Facility and Business Owners' Corner

- If you are new to the site or are just beginning to explore housing alternatives, take the guided tour. Here you will learn about all the different types of senior facilities available.

- If you know what you are looking for, click on either *Find a Facility Fast* or *Jump To the Hot Spots*. Each of these links allows you to search accommodations by health status among other criteria.

Other Sites

Extended Care Information Network

http://www.elderconnect.com/

- Search the database of 24,000 extended care providers and over 9,000 home health care agencies at this site.

Senior Living Home Page

http://www.seniorliving.com/

- This site provides extensive listings of residences and resources—such as travel deals and products—for active seniors.

Medical Advice

◆ Healthfinder
◆ Foundation for Osteoporosis Research and Education
◆ Menopause Online ◆ Ask Dr. Weil
◆ Dental ResourceNet ◆ Other Sites

The number of medical advice and resource sites is growing rapidly. The information in these sites is getting better and more accessible. Now you can find out about nutrition, hundreds of common first-aid solutions, and much more.

Healthfinder

http://www.healthfinder.org/default.htm

 If you are looking for health info, be sure that you go to reputable sites, like the Federal Department of Health and Human Services' Healthfinder.

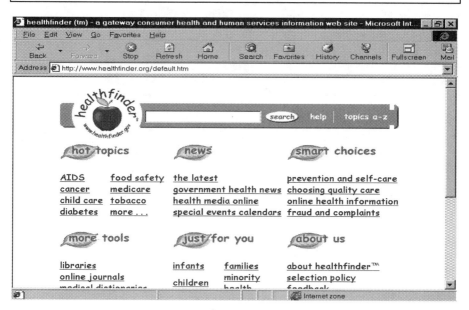

- Search by subject using the Healthfinder site. Topics include everything from the ordinary—such as the common cold—to the more obscure—such as the rare inherited vision disorder achromatopsia. Each topic links to a catalog of additional links, medical journals, support groups, and Government agencies.

- The site also provides excellent hot topic features that cover a variety of issues such as Medicare policies, food safety, and Alzheimer's disease.

- On the bottom of the home page, click the *senior* link to find senior-specific resources. The *Directory of Web Sites on Aging* link opens the door to additional wonderful senior sites. This is a great area to explore.

Directory of Web Sites on Aging

Sites by Subject/Topic	Organization Sites
Academic/Research Sites	International Sites
Other Aging Directories	Sites by State NEW

- The Healthfinder site is easy to navigate, full of important information, and interesting to explore. And, most importantly, you don't need to be a health care professional to understand the information on these pages.

Foundation for Osteoporosis Research and Education

http://www.fore.org/

Osteoporosis is a disease that effects over 25 million Americans. There are some simple dos and don'ts that can help you beat these odds. Check out this nonprofit, educational site for lots of information.

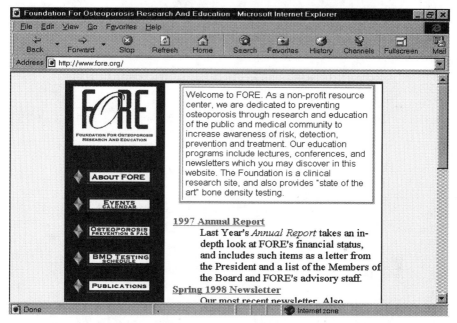

- The old adage an ounce of prevention is worth a pound of cure could be this site's motto. FORE stresses education about osteoporosis as a means to avoid getting this debilitating disease.

- Though many of the preventative measures need to be taken when you are young and your bones are developing, it is never too late to start good habits.

- This site provides an abundance of articles, information, FAQs (frequently asked questions), support for those with osteoporosis, and excellent health guidelines for those without.

Menopause Online

http://www.menopause-online.com/

 This site is dedicated to providing women (and the men who love them) support, strength, and up-to-date information about menopause.

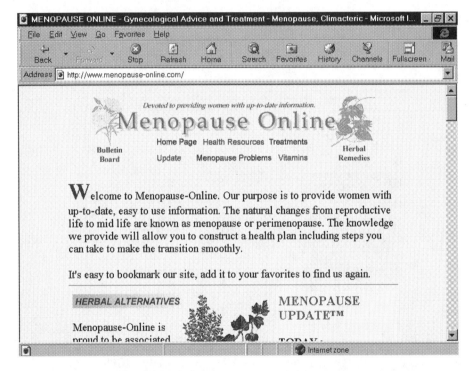

- This site focuses on integrative measures for dealing with the changes that a woman's body undergoes as she experiences menopause. This includes combining healthy diet and exercise with herbal remedies, vitamins, acupuncture, and homeopathy.

- Menopause online also features the latest scientific studies, health resources, and a bulletin board system where you can post questions or share your experiences, and more.

Ask Dr. Weil

www.drweil.com

 If you want to learn about healthy living or find the answer to a simple health-related question, this is good place to explore.

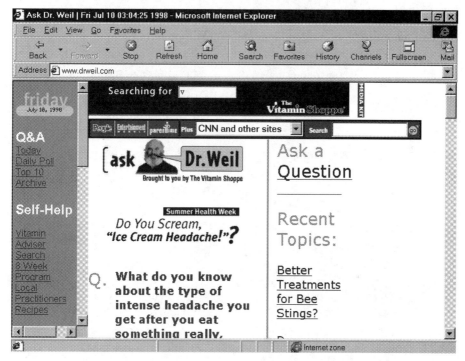

- Even if you don't have a health concern, exploring Dr. Weil's site can be informative and entertaining. The core of the site is Dr. Weil's responses to questions that are posted by visitors to the site.

- Go to the site to post a question or browse the archives.

- Most of the questions address common concerns like the best way to treat a sunburn or quick cures for a stomachache. If you are looking for data on a more serious ailment, you may want to try one of the other medical sites.

- Dr. Weil is an advocate of staying healthy through diet and exercise. He also supports trying natural remedies over strong prescription drugs.

- The information on the page, especially under the Self-Help heading, may sound a bit "new age." But it is all sound information. And if you like to cook, be sure to check out the healthy recipes.

Dental ResourceNet

http://www.dentalcare.com

Procter & Gamble's dental care site answers questions about everything essential to proper dental care and dental procedures.

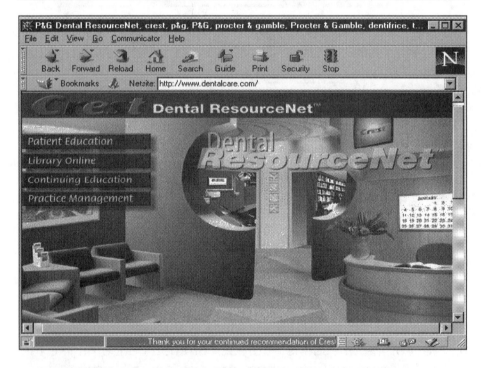

- The Procter & Gamble Crest Dental ResourceNet answers the most common questions about effective dental care. Although many areas on this site are primarily for the use of health care professionals who must register to access this information, there are many informative areas that are available to lay people.

■ While going to the dentist may be a frightening proposition, this site makes the most out of what may at first seem unappealing. Click on the *Patient Education* link to learn more about such topics as proper dental hygiene, wisdom tooth treatments, and root canals.

■ Click on the *Consumer Site* link to go to the P&G House Call area. Here you can find links to dental care for adults and seniors. Learn how osteoporosis and menopause affect your mouth, compare the benefits of dentures versus implants, read about high blood pressure concerns, and much more.

Other Sites

Mayo Health Oasis
http://www.mayohealth.org/

♦ Health, nutrition, and simple cures for ailments—it's all here at the Mayo Health Oasis. Click on the many links for valuable, free medical information.

Hypertension Network
http://www.bloodpressure.com/

♦ This site's aim is to disseminate information to the 50 million Americans (at least the ones who use the Internet) who suffer from high blood pressure.

OncoLink:
A University of Pennsylvania Cancer Center Resource
http://oncolink.upenn.edu/

♦ This online resource is devoted to the study of cancer, precautions to take, and how to live with the disease.

The Osteoporosis Center

http://www.endocrineweb.com/osteoporosis/

◆ This site provides excellent resources that make osteoporosis care and prevention easy to understand. Find detailed information on such key topics as maintenance of strong bones and the effect of menopause on bone strength.

MedAccess

http://www.medaccess.com/

◆ Here you can find links to the nation's best healthcare facilities as well as health and wellness topics and comprehensive healthcare information for senior citizens.

National Institute of Mental Health's Anxiety Disorders

http://www.nimh.nih.gov/anxiety

◆ The National Institute of Mental Health's Anxiety Disorders Education Program is a national campaign dedicated to educating the public and health care professionals about how to identify anxiety disorders and their effective treatments.

Yahoo! Health Topic Search Site

http://www.yahoo.com/Health/

◆ Almost any health questions you have can be answered at this site. Questions on environmental health, transplant resources, or fitness can be answered by clicking on the appropriate link.

Watching Your Money Grow

♦ Yahoo! Finance ♦ Morningstar
♦ The Street ♦ Other Sites

Using the Internet, you can follow your investments,
manage your portfolio, trade online, read expert trader
insight, and get fast-breaking news on financial trends. Best
of all, many of the sites include free services as well as top-
flight portfolio management for subscribers.

Yahoo! Finance

http://quote.yahoo.com/

 When Yahoo! launches a service, it's
guaranteed to be top-notch. The Yahoo!
Finance pages are a great place to find
financial information.

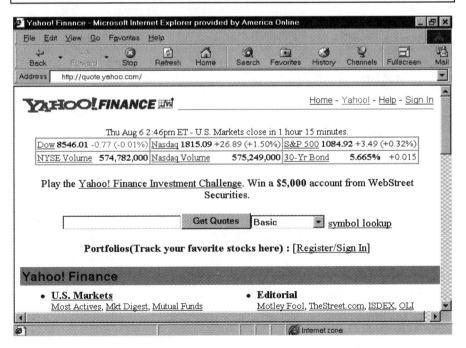

- What Yahoo! does best is organize information on the Web. The Finance pages are an excellent example of how well Yahoo! does its job. Go to the Finance home page for a directory of categories and subcategories all related to financial issues, news, and services. Main categories include U.S. Markets, World Markets, Loans, and Financial News.

- You can customize the Yahoo! financial page to display information that best suits your needs. To do so, click *Sign In* on the home page to register. Registration is free and easy. Then click the *Customize* link on the home page. The following customizable options are then displayed. Click on the areas you wish to customize.

Yahoo Account Information
Edit your Yahoo! personal information and change your password or email address. This information applies to all of Yahoo's free customizable features and will be kept strictly confidential.

News Headlines
Choose your news headlines sources and how the headlines are displayed.

Market Summary
Track major market indices (or your favorite stocks) on the top of quote pages.

Portfolios
Manage your portfolios: edit or delete existing portfolios, create new portfolios, or sort the order of your portfolios.

Quote Display
Configure quotes to display in fraction or decimal format, choose colors and how high/low limits are displayed when tripped.

Charts
Choose the default timeframe displayed on charts.

- To stay on top of the latest financial news, read the huge number of articles under the Latest Market News heading. Also, for the multilingual financier or international investor, Yahoo! financial pages can be accessed in French, Japanese, Swedish, and other languages. Just click on the desired link under World Finance.

Morningstar

http://www.morningstar.net

 Get the low-down on mutual fund and stock market investing from the leading mutual fund investment firm and its database of more than 6,500 funds and more than 8,000 stocks.

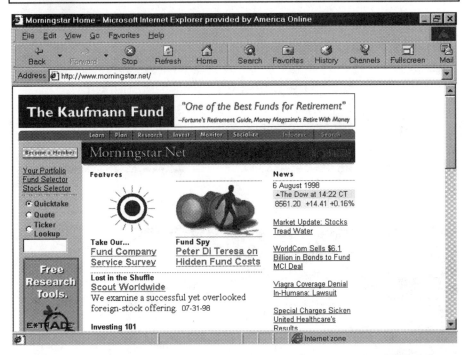

- Morningstar has made its name as the top provider of mutual fund data and analysis. Now you can have free access to the wealth of Morningstar investment research tools at the Morningstar site.

- The real gem here is the Data Screen tool. From the Morningstar home page, click on the *Stock Screens* or *Fund Screens* links. Next, select a stock sector or fund category from the lists provided. For example, you might want to find the ten best 3-year annualized returns for hybrid funds. Simply select those screening criteria and click to view the search results.

- Use the Monitor feature to check fund winners and losers on the current day's trading. Click the *Plan* link to review articles and features on preparing your investment strategy. You can also monitor up to ten portfolios using the Morningstar site.

- This complete investing tool also includes a Learn page with links to news, articles, and expert advice on building and managing your own portfolio.

The Street

http://www.thestreet.com

 Visit The Street for irreverent market commentary and analysis from a staff of Wall Street veterans with unfailing objectivity.

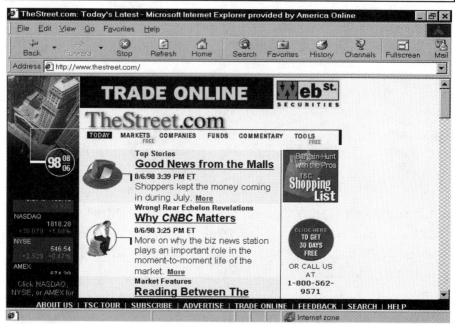

- Imagine you have round-the-clock access to the investment insight of a staff of top market analysts. Imagine that it costs you only about $9.95 a month (or $99.95 a year). Now stop imagining and go to The Street.

- The Street offers the analysis of leading Wall Street columnists and editors such as James J. Cramer, a hedge fund manager and a founder of *SmartMoney* magazine. The Street combines insider expertise and analysis with strict disclosure and objectivity standards— no staff reporters or editors can own stocks or positions except for mutual funds.

- In addition to market news and analysis, The Street offers an opinionated early morning e-mail roundup of company news, market developments, mutual fund coverage, and analyst columns called Daily Bulletin.

- If you don't want the full range of Street services, you can still log on to The Street for free to get daily market news and access some services such as Lipper Analyticals Fund Facts and Scoreboards.

Other Sites

Douglas Gerlach's Invest-O-Rama
http://www.investorama.com/

- With more than 81,000 links on 89 categories, Geralach's site is the largest financial resource on the Internet. Among the many features of the Invest-O-Rama site is the Ask Doug feature where you can e-mail Gerlach financial questions or read the archives. You can also subscribe to a free monthly newsletter.

The Motley Fool Finance and Folly
http://www.motleyfool.com/

- This financial site is not for everyone. The site operates like a financial cooperative, where everyone—both experts and financial laymen— can offer financial advice, tips, and share his or her experiences. The site's mission is "to instruct, to amuse, and to make you good money."

Extra! Extra! Read All About It!

◆ **The New York Times on the Web**
◆ **CNN Interactive** ◆ **Other Sites**

Keep on top of the day's breaking stories. In addition to headline news, you can check out feature articles on fashion, movies, political cartoons, and more. Get up-to-the-minute information online 24 hours a day.

The New York Times on the Web

http://www.nytimes.com/

"All the news That's Fit To Print" is posted by these news-distribution giants. Updated every 10 minutes, *The New York Times* site brings you all the news, all the time.

- To begin using this mammoth site, you must first register. Registering is free and quick to do.

- Once you've registered, select a news section, such as Front Page or Sports, click on a headline to read an article, or click on *News by Category* to see headings that include international, national, metro, style, arts, and a photo gallery. From most articles you can access related articles and/or online forums. From Front Page you can click to read quick summaries of the day's top news stories.

- Click on *CyberTimes* to access all breaking technological news as well as archived articles. This page also posts an excellent Internet glossary, other news, views, and resources related to the electronic age.

- For up-to-the-minute news, select AP Breaking News for the hottest stories. The features on this page are updated every ten minutes.

CNN Interactive

http://www.cnn.com/

Get all the news you need from the worldwide leader in cable television news. You can also access more than 100 other sources, such as CNNSI, a collaboration between CNN and Sports Illustrated.

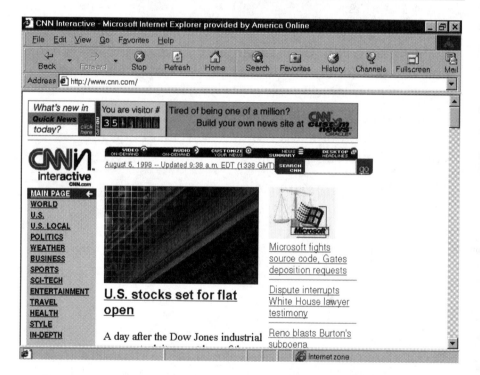

- The CNN cable news network is widely recognized as a world leader in news reporting, so it comes as no surprise that the CNN Interactive Web site is as feature- and content-rich as the 24-hour news network's television coverage.

- The CNN Interactive site brings together CNN's own newsgathering team and the content of more than 100 other magazines and news outlets.

- The CNN Interactive home page presents the day's headlines with links to full stories. You can also click on news topics of interest, including *World, US, Local, Weather, Sports, Sci-Tech, Style, Travel, Showbiz, Health,* and *Earth.*

- From the home page you can link to *CNNfn* for financial and business news, *CNNSI* for sports news, and *allpolitics* for political coverage.

- Scroll down the home page to view a complete directory of CNN Interactive site links, including direct links to stories under main heading categories.

Other Sites

MSNBC

http://www.msnbc.com

- ♦ Quickly scan daily news headlines or read the news in more detail. From this site, you can also access CNBC, MSNBC, and NBC television news.

International Herald Tribune

http://www.iht.com/IHT/home.html

- ♦ A true world newspaper, the International Herald Tribune's Web site is a great place to keep on top of world events.

NewsWorks

http://www.newsworks.com

- ♦ Get the day's news from more than 130 major U.S. newspaper Web sites.

Online Magazines

◆ Senior News Network by SeniorCom

Keep up-to-date on current events, trends, fashions, music reviews, and more without having to stop at the local newsstand. Many e-zines (electronic magazines) are geared towards the 50+ crowd.

Senior News Network by SeniorCom

http://www.seniornews.com/

 Senior News Network is like an online newsstand that lets you access dozens of e-zines from one location.

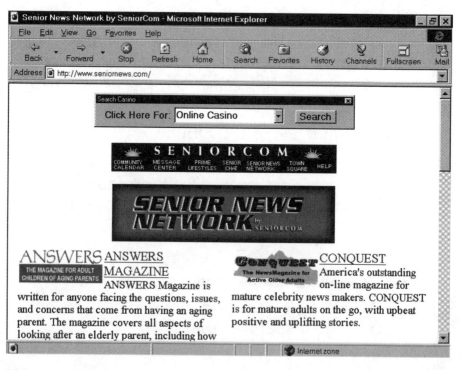

- From the Senior News Network home page you can link to over a dozen online magazines. Be sure to bookmark magazines that you like so that you can easily return to read the latest issue.

- Following is a brief description of each magazine featured on the Senior News Network home page.

- **ANSWERS Magazine**

  - This magazine is written for children responsible for an elder parent. Field specialists contribute articles dealing with such topics as legal rights, housing, coping, depression, elder abuse, and more.

  - In addition to the online magazine, you can subscribe to a printed, bimonthly version of the magazine. Subscriptions are not free.

- **Grand Times Magazine**

  - This online magazine provides "controversial, entertaining, and informative" content for active older adults.

  - Updated weekly, this e-zine features a terrific area called Making Sense, which discusses financial issues. Also be sure to read the articles in Lifestyles, where seniors reflect on and share their experiences.

- **Colorado Life**

  - ◆ If you plan to visit Colorado, you live there, or you are just interested in information about this state, explore the abundance of information in this e-zine. This online magazine is an offshoot of the e-zine Maturity USA.

- **Senior Beacon**

  - ◆ This site explores the emerging changes in society as seniors become the largest growing section of our population.

- **Senior Magazine**

  - ◆ This site features editorials and special articles in addition to the "usual suspects": health tips, chat areas, travel information, and more.

- **Southern California Senior Life**

  - ◆ The name says it all: this site provides senior-biased information for residents of Southern California.

- **Conquest**

  - ◆ This online magazines that caters to on-the-go seniors has a celebrity news slant. Read bios and stories about famous seniors including such diverse stars as Soupy Sales and Joan Rivers.

  - ◆ Also be sure to check out this site's excellent financial information.

- **Maryland Maturity Lifestyles**

  - ◆ If you are a high-income resident of Maryland or you plan to vacation there and you are an active senior between the ages of 50-65, then this site will be right up your alley. Otherwise, stick with the numerous other available e-zines.

  - ◆ Though you can find information on general areas of interest, Maryland Lifestyle articles focus primarily on leisure-related activities.

- **New Choices**

- ◆ This great-looking site is the online version of Reader's Digest magazine with the same name. You can subscribe to the magazine at the site. Subscriptions are not free.

- ◆ Reader's Digest's site provides a wonderful variety of news, travel information, relationship views, and more.

- **Senior Connection**

- ◆ This site, originating in Florida, provides content for all seniors, but focuses on resources for seniors in West Central Florida.

- **SNN Global Edition**

- ◆ Senior News Network's Global Edition posts hot news and contemporary views.

- ◆ If you have an article that you wish to have published, click the *let us know!* link on the Senior News Network home page. The link opens a blank, pre-addressed e-mail message for you to contact the site's editor.

Newsgroups

◆ Deja News
◆ Accessing Newsgroups through Your ISP
◆ Newsgroup Categories ◆ Rules of the Road

A Newsgroup is on ongoing discussion on a particular topic. Newsgroup members post messages, often called articles, to contribute to the discussion. You can find Newsgroups in an area of the Internet called Usenet.

Newsgroups, also known as Discussion Groups, work like an enormous electronic bulletin board—you can post questions, respond to someone else's question, or just share your expertise. Discussion groups are not chat sites; they are databases of messages.

Though Newsgroups may seem a little bit intimidating at first, they can offer a huge amount of invaluable information. Some would argue that Newsgroups are the most important area of the Internet.

Newsgroups can be accessed many different ways, but using the Deja News site is the easiest place to start.

Deja News

http://www.dejanews.com/

Deja News, which houses more than 50,000 discussion forums, is a great place to meet people with the same interests or to find information on most any topic.

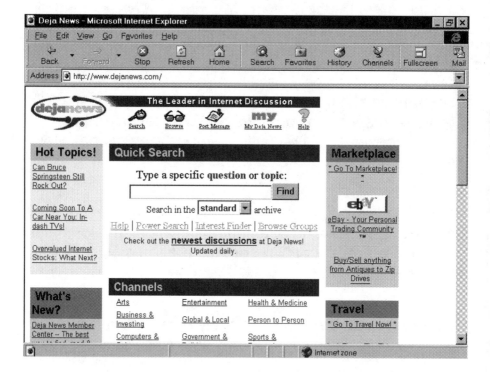

- To get started at the Deja News site, click on the *Help* link on the home page, then click the *Help Wizard* for tutorials on many basic Deja News tools and features.

> For an overview of our main features, click on the feature you want to learn more about. In just a few clicks you should arrive a an answer to your question.
>
> ## Show me help on:
>
> **• Searching**
> [Frequently Asked Questions]
> [Search Language]
>
> **• Posting**
> [Frequently Asked Questions]
> [Posting Rules and Information]
>
> **• Browse Groups**
>
> **• Deja News Categories**
>
> **• Usenet in General**
> [Frequently Asked Questions]
>
> **• My Deja News**

- From the Help page you can also explore Deja News FAQs (frequently asked questions) and Deja News search options.

- To find an article or Newsgroup:

  - Type one or more search keyword—a question or topic—in the Quick Search text box on the home page.

  - To narrow your search you can select *standard*, *complete*, *adult*, *jobs*, or *for sale* from the Search in drop-down list. Or, select from the Channels to search. Selecting one of these options will narrow your results.

  - Click **Find**.

  - To browse through the list of found articles, click the desired hyperlink.

- For example, a search on the keywords *senior citizens* turned up 1,251 results—some of the results were completely unrelated, but many included articles on Web sites for seniors and senior discounts.

- In order to reply to an article, you need to first register with Deja News. Deja News requires registration so that they can filter out users who post inappropriate material or don't follow Newsgroup netiquette (network etiquette).

- After reading an article, you can post a reply or new message that anyone can read, or you can reply directly to the author by e-mail.

- Registration also sets up My Deja News. With My Deja News you can subscribe to favorite Newsgroups. You can also establish a free e-mail account so that you won't need to worry about inundating your regular e-mail account with messages or spam (computer junk mail).

Accessing Newsgroups through Your ISP

 Though accessing Newsgroups is easiest with Deja News, more options may be available to you if you access them with your news server.

- Most ISPs provide access to Newsgroups through a news server. You will have to configure your browser or Internet program so that it will know the location of your ISP news server. You do this in the same way you configured the browser to find your ISP mail server.

- Below you will find a list of browsers and their corresponding Newsgroups:
  - Netscape Communicator: **Netscape Collabra**
  - Internet Explorer: **Outlook Express**
  - America Online: **keyword: Newsgroups**

- Configuring your news server will not be covered in this book. You may need to contact your Internet Service Provider for information on setting up your news server.

Newsgroup Categories

 When you first see a list of Newsgroups, the Newsgroup names may not appear to be related to the content of the group. Once you understand a little about naming conventions used in Newsgroups, you will find your way around easily.

- Newsgroup name extensions identify the category. The list of categories is incomplete. Some servers will have more categories.

  - **alt.** and **misc.**
    Anything not covered in other groups

  - **comp.**
    Computers

  - **news.**
    Information about Newsgroups, such as FAQ lists for individual groups, netiquette, updates, and information on how to get started with Newsgroups

  - **rec.**
    Recreational topics, such as hobbies and entertainment

  - **sci.**
    Science

  - **soc.**
    Social issues

  - **talk.**
    Opinions on any topic

Rules of the Road

 A message that you post can have a potential audience of millions. Therefore, it's important that you follow a few basic guidelines.

- Most Newsgroup sites have a FAQs (frequently asked questions) section that pertains to that group. When you visit a new Newsgroup, this is the first place you should go. Questions include specific posting rules.

- Read through past entries to get a sense of the group. Different groups on the same topic may have very different attitudes towards a topic. This will help you keep in sync with the other members. Or, you may find that this is not the Newsgroup for you.

- Stick to the subject.

- Be sure that your message will not be misunderstood. If you are at all worried that it may be misinterpreted, add a few emoticons to emphasize your tone. (See **Appendix B**.)

- Try to keep messages to a manageable length.

- Chain letters or pyramid schemes are illegal. Never post one at a Newsgroup or anywhere else on the Internet. Also, never post any type of solicitation for commercial products.

- Avoid cross-posting messages. This is when you post the same message to several Newsgroups. When you cross-post a message, chances are the message won't be appropriate for all the groups that will view your message. Keep your messages group-specific.

Mailing Lists

◆ Liszt ◆ Yahoo! Mailing Lists
◆ Rules of the Road ◆ Other Sites

Like Newsgroups (see **Newsgroups**), Mailing Lists aren't live. Mailing Lists are made up of participants who discuss certain topics via e-mail.

To participate in a Mailing List, you must first subscribe to the list and then all postings are e-mailed to you. If you have something to say, simply send an e-mail to the list's address. The message is then forwarded to all the members of the group. Or, if you wish to respond to someone else's posting, just click your e-mail's Reply button, type your message, click Send, and the entire Mailing List group will receive your comments.

One note of warning: when you subscribe to a Mailing List, you may receive hundreds of e-mail messages daily. Most of the e-mails will be pertinent to the Mailing List topic, but inevitably, people will start private conversations. It can be frustrating at times sifting through all of the e-mail. Luckily, you can unsubscribe to a Mailing List just as easily as you can subscribe to one.

Liszt

http://liszt.com/

Lizst, an enormous Mailing List directory that maintains a catalog of more than 80,000 lists, is the place to begin exploring the world of Mailing Lists.

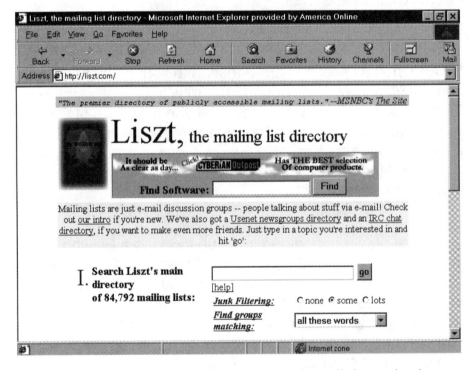

- If you are new to lists, click the *our intro* link on the home page. The intro is a brief list of the basics: what a Mailing List is, what Liszt is, etc.

- From the Intro page, click on the *Help With Liszt* link for the nitty-gritty on getting started with Mailing Lists. Included here is information on conducting Mailing List searches.

- From the home page you can begin by doing your own search. Selecting *none* as the Junk Filtering option will give you more matches (and more junk), whereas selecting *lots* will turn up more selective results.

- For example, a search on the word *seniors* generated 21 lists, including seniors interested in arts and seniors interested in computers.

- You can also click on one of the Liszt categories to search for a list.

II. **...or click on any topic to browse *Liszt Select*:**

Arts (175 lists)
Literature, Television, Movies ...

Business (149 lists)
Finance, Jobs, Marketing ...

Computers (238 lists)
Internet, Database, Programming ...

Culture (263 lists)
Gay, Jewish, Parenting ...

Education (103 lists)
Distance_Education, Academia, Internet ...

Health (255 lists)
Medicine, Allergy, Support ...

Humanities (233 lists)
Philosophy, History, Psychology ...

Music (195 lists)
Bands, Singer-Songwriters, Genres ...

Nature (113 lists)
Animals, Environment, Plants ...

News (40 lists)
International, Regional, Politics ...

Politics (86 lists)
Environment, Activism, Human_Rights ...

Recreation (342 lists)
Games, Autos, Sports ...

Religion (96 lists)
Christian, Jewish, Women ...

Science (95 lists)

Social (87 lists)

- If you find a list that interests you, click the link next to the list's name. Here you can read additional information about the list and, if you wish, follow the prompts to subscribe.

- You can also search on Usenet and IRC Chat Channels (real-time chat) from the Liszt search pages.

Yahoo! Mailing Lists

http://search.yahoo.com/bin/search?p=mailing+lists

 The Yahoo! search engine has a large selection of Mailing Lists. To access these lists either enter the URL above, or type *mailing lists* in the Yahoo! Search box and press Enter.

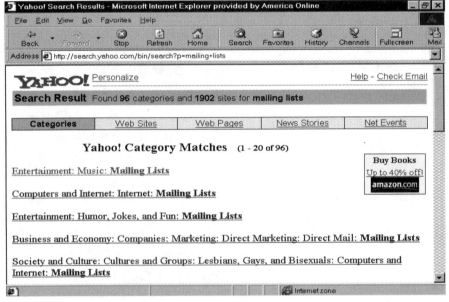

- The nice thing about accessing Mailing Lists through Yahoo!, is that many Mailing Lists maintain their own Web page. When you subscribe to a Mailing List using Yahoo!, you go through the list's home page. Many such home pages include additional information and other resources.

- The Yahoo! catalog of Mailing Lists contains almost 2,000 main topics, all of which contain a variety of lists.

- If you find that you enjoy participating in Mailing Lists, do a search on the words *Mailing Lists* at different search engines to see what you find. But, for sanity's sake, avoid subscribing to too many lists—unless you like spending your time sorting through lots and lots of e-mail.

Rules of the Road

You must abide by a few simple formalities if you wish to participate in Mailing Lists.

- See **Rules of the Road** for **Newsgroups**, page 206. All of these conventions apply to Mailing Lists as well.

Other Sites

Publicly Accessible Mailing Lists

http://www.neosoft.com/internet/paml/index.html

- ◆ Just as the name implies, this is a catalog of Mailing Lists.

Tile.net-Lists

http://tile.net/lists/

- ◆ At this site you can search for Mailing Lists and Newsgroups.

Internet Mailing Lists Guides and Resources

http://www.nlc-bnc.ca/ifla/I/training/listserv/lists.htm

- ◆ In addition to Mailing List search features, this site provides an illustrated explanation of how Mailing Lists work.

Computer Savvy Seniors

◆ Seniors Helping Seniors ◆ SeniorNet ◆ Other Sites

As a senior, you are part of the fastest-growing demographic group to explore the ever-changing Internet. Whether you're just getting your feet wet in the world of communication technology or you're sailing smoothly online, you know there is always more to learn. The Internet contains numerous sites that are dedicated to adults who are interested in discovering more about the world of technology.

Seniors Helping Seniors

http://www.ageofreason.com/help.htm

 Computer-savvy senior volunteers share their time, knowledge, and e-mail to help those new to computers and the Internet.

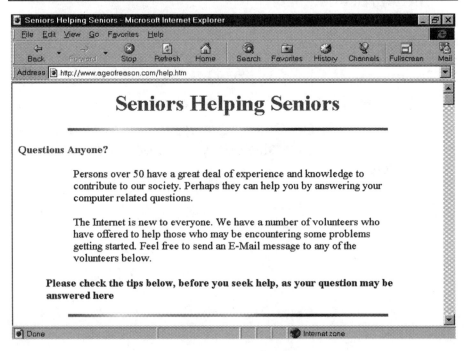

Seniors Helping Seniors - Microsoft Internet Explorer

File Edit View Go Favorites Help

Back   Forward   Stop   Refresh   Home   Search   Favorites   History   Channels   Fullscreen   Mail

Address http://www.ageofreason.com/help.htm

Seniors Helping Seniors

Questions Anyone?

Persons over 50 have a great deal of experience and knowledge to contribute to our society. Perhaps they can help you by answering your computer related questions.

The Internet is new to everyone. We have a number of volunteers who have offered to help those who may be encountering some problems getting started. Feel free to send an E-Mail message to any of the volunteers below.

Please check the tips below, before you seek help, as your question may be answered here

Done   Internet zone

- The Seniors Helping Seniors pages are straightforward and easy to navigate. You'll find general Internet tips as well as expert advice from senior volunteers.

- Each senior expert has a specific forte. You will find general computer specialists, as well as software and Internet experts. Click on an expert volunteer's name to open a blank e-mail message. Enter your inquiry and click *Send.*

- At the bottom of the page click on *More Tips on Computer Operating Systems And Applications* for additional pointers.

SeniorNet

http://www.seniornet.org/

 SeniorNet's mission is to help older adults join the telecommunications revolution through education and training.

- One of the most helpful and interesting features of the SeniorNet site is their online message board. Using the message boards, you can post questions or share your knowledge and others can then respond.

- Unlike chats, message boards are not live (see **Newsgroups**). They're like electronic bulletin boards. The forum is for everyone—computer novices as well as pros—who wishes to discuss technology with others.

- Before you can participate you must register with SeniorNet. Registration is free and only takes a few minutes to do. Once registered, be sure to explore the other message boards in addition to the technology-related ones.

- Maneuvering the message boards is easy to do once you get the hang of it. But first, you should read the How to use the RoundTables, Introductions, and Newcomers Help postings.

- In addition to online services, SeniorNet has 137 Learning Centers in operation and new centers are opening every month. The Learning Centers offer low-cost, low-pressure training for older adults.

Other Sites

Internet Help Desk

http://w3.one.net/~alward/

- Find troubleshooting tips, links to tools, Web guides, consulting services, and more at this free service site.

Help-Site.com

http://help-site.com/

- Search this computer site for information on a wide range of technical categories—including hardware, software, and the Internet.

URL Troubleshooting: Addressee Unknown

Web sites change or go out of business every day. Files are located on Web servers all over the world and sometimes the location of these files change. It can be frustrating to access information one day, but the next day find that the file is no longer available or that the site has moved with no forwarding address.

Following are a few tips and explanations of common types of connection errors that you may encounter. Wording of the error messages may vary.

What is a URL?

 URL stands for Uniform Resource Locator, the Web address. It is a command used within the World Wide Web system to hunt for linked sites.

- Check the URL you have entered carefully:
  - It's very easy to type one wrong letter or symbol. This may not seem like a big deal but, in fact, it may be the reason you can't connect to the site you want.
  - URLs—especially the long complex addresses—must be typed exactly. That includes correct spelling and punctuation.
  - In addition, pay attention to upper- and lowercase letters. Sometimes computer servers are case-sensitive and will not understand a name entered in lowercase when it should be capitalized.

Error: The Server Does Not Have a DNS Entry

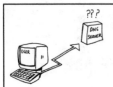 A DNS error may be caused if you have incorrectly typed the URL or if the Web site has moved or changed addresses.

- DNS is an acronym for Domain Name Service.

- After you enter a Web address, the computer first converts the URL into a series of numbers—the protocol that computers understand. If you look at your Status bar as you try to connect to a site, you'll see these numbers. The computer then attempts to locate the address.

- When you get a DNS error, first double-check to make sure that you have entered the URL correctly.

- Sometimes the server that houses the Web site is down, so don't give up on a site right away. Try accessing the site later.

Error: 404 Not Found

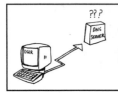 The page that you have entered could not be located.

- If you receive this error, several things may have happened. The file name may have changed, the server name may have changed, or you may have typed a spelling error in the URL.

- In many cases it's just a matter of trying the address again. There may be a great deal of Web traffic to the site or congestion on your browser server. Try the same address a couple times.

- Try backtracking to the home page to see if the site is still active. Simply remove all information to the right of the first single slash. It could be that the page still exists, but its location within the Web site has changed. For example, in the following URL:

http://www.ddcpub.com/html/win98VRB.html
(a page on the DDC Publishing Web site),

delete everything after *.com/*. This will take you to the DDC home page.

Error: Forbidden - You don't have permission to access on this server
OR
401-Unauthorized
OR
403-Forbidden

 Some Web sites or pages of a Web site require passwords for access.

- If you have a password for the site, check to see if you entered it correctly.

- If you don't have a password, explore the page to see if there is a place to register to receive a password. If there is no area for registration, you will be unable to go to the site.

Error: Spinning Hourglass or Beachball

A connection is being made, but the page is either taking a very long time to load or a router, or path, is disabled.

- If you have spent much time on the Internet, you've learned that patience is the key to success. Sometimes there is just too much traffic on the site or a temperamental server may be down.
- Try the site later or try refreshing or reloading the site.

Error: 503-Service Unavailable

This error is usually caused by too much traffic to the site.

- There is only one solution to this error: try again later. If too many people attempt access to a site at the same time, a traffic jam occurs. Sometimes it's best to pull off the information highway and take a break at a rest stop.

Error: A connection with the server could not be established

This could mean one of several things: the site could be experiencing technical difficulty or it could be no longer in operation.

- When you see this message, you should try again later. If you keep trying with no results, try doing a search on the site's name to see if the page still exists.

Support Resources

The Internet provides valuable resources that help you deal with coping, depression, loss, and more. Perhaps the best thing about exploring these sites is simply the reassurance that you are not alone.

Bereavement and Hospice Support Netline

http://ube.ubalt.edu/www/bereavement/ index.htmlx

- This site provides a directory, organized by state, of bereavement support groups, services, and hospice bereavement programs.

If You're Over 65 and Feeling Depressed...

http://www.nimh.nih.gov/publicat/over65.htm

- Depression is a clinical condition that effects millions of Americans every year. The information at this site focuses on the different types of depression, causes of depression, and additional support resources.

Before I Die Home Page

http://www.pbs.org/wnet/bid/

- As the online component of the PBS series *Before I Die: Medical Care and Personal Choices*, this site focuses on "medical, ethical, and social issues surrounding end-of-life care in America today."

WidowNet

http://www.fortnet.org/WidowNet/

- Here you will find self-help resources created by widows and widowers dedicated to all those who have lost a significant other.

National Hospice Organization

http://www.nho.org//

- This non-profit organization is devoted to increasing the awareness of and accessibility to hospice care.

Hospice Hands

http://hospice-cares.com/

- This site provides extensive articles, hospice indices, links, and other hospice resources.

Homecare Industry

http://www.ptct.com/html/industry.html

- Organized by state, this site catalogs hospices and homecare providers.

Links to Hospice Sites

http://www.teleport.com/~hospice/links.htm

- Here you will find links to hospice providers as well as general hospice information, facts, and articles.

Appendix A: Emoticons and Abbreviations

Since you cannot see the people with whom you communicate on the Internet, here are some symbols you can use to convey emotion in your messages. This section also contains some acronyms that you will encounter in Internet messages (such as e-mail, newsgroup messages, and chat room discussions). Be sure to use these cute symbols and abbreviations *only* in your personal communications.

For more emoticons and acronyms, go to the Emoticons & Smileys page:

http://home.earthlink.net/~gripweeds/emoticon.htm

Emoticons

■ Use these symbols to convey emotions in your messages. To see the faces in these symbols, turn the page to the right.

>:->	Angry	:-(	Sad
5:-)	Elvis	:-@	Scream
:-)	Happy	:-#	Secret (lips are sealed)
()	Hug	:P	Sticking Tongue Out
:-D	Joking	:-O	Surprised
:*	Kiss	:-J	Tongue in Cheek
:/)	Not Funny	;-)	Wink

Acronyms

- Listed below are some of the more-common acronyms, but new acronyms are always being created. Be sure to check online to see what's new.

ADN	Any day now	GMTA	Great minds think alike
ASAP	As soon as possible	IAE	In any event
B4N	Bye for now	IMO	In my opinion
BRB	Be right back	IRL	In real life
BTW	By the way	JIC	Just in case
DTRT	Do the right thing	LOL	Laugh out loud
F2F	Face to face	ROTFL	Rolling on the floor laughing
FAQ	Frequently asked questions	RTM	Read the manual
FWIW	For what it's worth	TIA	Thanks in advance
FYI	For your information	WFM	Works for me

Appendix B: Netiquette

Netiquette is the art of civilized communications between people on the Internet. Whenever you send an e-mail message, a chat room message, or a newsgroup message follow these guidelines.

A Few Tips

- Always include a subject in the message heading. This makes it easy for the recipient to organize messages in folders by topic and to find a message by browsing through message headers.

- Do not use capital letters. To the recipient, it feels like YOU ARE SHOUTING. Instead, enclose text that you want to emphasize with asterisks. For example: I *meant* Friday of *next* week.

- Be careful with the tone you use. With the absence of inflection, it is easy to send a message that can be misinterpreted by the recipient. Use emoticons to establish your intent. A smiley emoticon can make it clear to the recipient that you are really joking.

- Spell check your messages before you send them. They represent you.

- Do not send flame messages. These are obnoxious, offensive, or otherwise disturbing messages. If you send this type of message to a newsgroup, 30,000 people who read your flame will think less of you. If you receive flame mail, probably the best thing you can do is press the Delete button rather than the Reply button.

- Messages sent over the Internet are not private. Your message is in writing and nothing can prevent someone from forwarding it to anyone they please. Assume that anyone with a computer has the potential to read your message.

- If you send a long message, it is a good idea to tell the recipient at the beginning of the message so that they can decide if they would rather download it to read later.

- Never initiate or forward a chain letter. Some service providers will cancel your membership if you do so, as they are trying to protect their members from unwanted mail.

The Netiquette Home Page

http://www.albion.com/netiquette/index.html

- This page lists hyperlinks to pages on Netiquette contributed by Internet users. You will find interesting, amusing, and very important material in these sites.

Appendix C: Timesaving Tools

◆ Financial Calculators ◆ Calculators Online
◆ Universal Currency Converter
◆ The Time Zones Page ◆ Naval Clock
◆ Fast Area Code Finder
◆ National Address and Zip+4 Browser

Use the Web tools listed here to save time by finding the answer to many common financial and mathematical questions. You can also get the correct time around the world with the Time Zones and Naval Clock sites.

Financial Calculators

- Have you ever wondered whether you should lease or purchase a car? How much money do you have to save to become a millionaire by the time you retire? How much rent can you afford?

- The financial calculators available at the Financial Calculators page of the TimeValue Software Web site provide a host of interesting and practical tools for finding the answer to your financial questions.

- The directory of calculator links includes categories such as Auto Loans & Leasing, Loans & Savings Calculators, General Financial Calculators, Mortgage Calculators, Insurance Calculators, Tax Calculators, and Just For Fun Calculators.

Calculators Online

http://www-sci.lib.uci.edu/HSG/RefCalculators.html

- Another calculator site at Martindale's "The Reference Desk" provides more than 5,300 calculators.

- Links to the calculators are arranged in an alphabetical index of categories and subtopics. Click on a link to use one of the calculators.

- Business categories include Home & Office, Finance, Management/Business, Insurance, Stocks, Bonds, Options, and Commodities & Futures.

- You can also find many calculators for practical matters such as clothing, arts and crafts, medical, and law. Numerous mathematics and science calculators are also available, from simple unit conversion calculators to astrophysics.

Universal Currency Converter

http://www.xe.net./currency/

- This simple and useful Web site does one thing only, but does it well—currency conversion. If, for example, you want to know how many French francs you can get for $100, turn to this Web page.

- Type the amount of currency you want to convert, then select the type of currency (e.g., U.S. dollars). Next, select the type of currency you're converting to (e.g., French francs), and click the Perform Currency Conversion button.

- The Currency Converter tells you that $100 converts to 596.90 French francs. (Note that currency exchange rates fluctuate and converting currency usually requires a fee.)

The Time Zone Page

http://www.west.net/~lindley/zone/

- Another simple but very useful site is the Time Zone Page. Find the current time for more than 600 cities around the world.

- Select a city from the menu, then click Get the Time!

Naval Clock

http://tycho.usno.navy.mil/cgi-bin/timer.pl

- To check the most accurate clock available, go to the Naval Clock Web site. The site displays the current time in all North American time zones as well as Universal Time (also called Greenwich Mean Time).

Fast Area Code Finder

http://www.555-1212.com/aclookup.html

- Find an area code fast at this handy site. Simply enter a city name and/or click on a state from the drop-down list menu, then click Get Area Code! If you know the area code but want to find where the code serves, type the area code in the Area Code text box and click Get Location.

National Address and ZIP+4 Browser

http://www.semaphorecorp.com/cgi/form.html

- If you need to look up a Zip Code, go to this site and enter the company name plus as much of its address as you know. The Zip Browser returns the complete, correct address, including the correct 9-digit Zip Code. Great for cleaning up old mailing lists.

Glossary

Listed below and on the following pages are terms that you may encounter on your Internet travels.

address book A place where frequently used e-mail addresses are stored.

anonymous FTP A special kind of FTP service that allows any user to log on. Anonymous FTP sites have a predefined user named "anonymous" that accepts any password.

Archie A database system of FTP resources. It helps you find files that exist anywhere on the Internet.

ARPAnet (Advanced Research Projects Administration Network) Ancestor to the Internet: ARPAnet began in 1969 as a project developed by the US Department of Defense. Its initial purpose was to enable researchers and military personnel to communicate in the event of an emergency.

ASCII file (American Standard Code for Information Interchange) File containing ASCII-formatted text only; can be read by almost any computer or program in the world.

attachment File(s) or Web pages(s) enclosed with an e-mail message.

Base64 (MIME) encoding One of the encoding schemes, used in the MIME (Multipurpose Internet Mail Extensions) protocol.

binary file A file containing machine language (that is, ones and zeros) to indicate that the file is more than plain text. A binary file must be encoded (converted to ASCII format) before it can be passed through the e-mail system.

BinHex An encoding scheme for the Macintosh platform that allows a file to be read as text when passed through the e-mail system.

Bookmark A browser feature that memorizes and stores the path to a certain Web site. Creating bookmarks enables a quick return to favorite sites.

browser A graphic interface program that helps manage the process of locating information on the World Wide Web. Browser programs such as Netscape Navigator and Microsoft Internet Explorer provide simple searching techniques and create paths that can return you to sites you visited previously.

chat (Internet Relay Chat) A live "talk" session with other Internet or network users in which a conversation is exchanged back and forth.

client program A computer program designed to talk to a specific server program. The FTP client program is designed to ask for and use the FTP service offered by an FTP server program. Client programs usually run in your own computer, and talk to server programs in the computers it connects to.

client A computer that is signing onto another computer. The computer that is logging on acts as the client; the other computer acts as the server.

complex search Uses two or more words in a text string (and may also use operators that modify the search string) to search for matches in a search engine's catalog.

compressed file A file that has been made smaller (without lost data) by using a file compression program such as pkzip or Stufflt. Compressed files are easier to send across the Internet, as they take less time to upload and download.

copyright The legal right of ownership of published material. E-mail messages are covered by copyright laws. In most cases, the copyright owner is the writer of the message.

crawlers Another name for search engines.

directories Also referred to as folders. Directories are lists of files and other directories. They are used for organizing and storing computer files.

domain The portion of an Internet address that follows the @ symbol and identifies the computer you are logging onto.

downloading Copying files (e-mail, software, documents, etc.) from a remote computer to your own computer.

e-mail (electronic mail) A communication system for exchanging messages and attached files. E-mail can be sent to anyone in the world as long as both parties have access to the Internet and an Internet address to identify themselves.

encoding A method of converting a binary file to ASCII format for e-mail purposes. Common encoding schemes include Uuencoding and MIME (Base64) encoding.

fair use The right to use short quotes and excerpts from copyrighted material such as e-mail messages.

FAQ (Frequently Asked Questions document) A text document that contains a collection of frequently asked questions about a particular subject. FAQs on many subjects are commonly available on the Web.

file "File" is a general term usually used to describe a computer document. It may also be used to refer to more than one file, however, such as groups of documents, software, games, etc.

folders/ directories Folders, also referred to as directories, are organized storage areas for maintaining computer files. Like filing cabinets, they help you manage your documents and files.

font A typeface that contains particular style and size specifications.

freeware Software that can be used for free forever. No license is required and the software may be copied and distributed legally.

FTP (File Transfer Protocol) The method of remotely transferring files from one computer to another over a network (or across the Internet). It requires that both the client and server computers use special communication software to talk to one another.

FTP site An Internet site that uses File Transfer Protocol and enables files to be downloaded and/or uploaded. When you access an FTP site through a browser application, however, your log-in is considered "anonymous" and will not allow uploading.

FTP (File Transfer Protocol) A computer program used to move files from one computer to another. The FTP program usually comes in two parts: a server program that runs in the computers offering the FTP service, and a client program running in computers, like yours, that wish to use the service.

Gopher A menu system that allows you to search various sources available on the Internet. It is a browsing system that works much like a directory or folder. Each entry may contain files and/or more directories to dig through.

heading fields (headings) Individual fields, like To and From, in the header of an e-mail message.

hierarchically structured catalog A catalog of Web sites that is organized into a few major categories that have sub-categories under them. Each sub-category has additional sub-categories under it. The level of detail in this structure depends on the particular Web site.

home page A Web site's starting point. A home page is like a table of contents. It outlines what a particular site has to offer, and usually contains connecting links to other related areas of the Internet as well.

host A central computer that other computers log onto for the purpose of sharing and exchanging information.

hot lists Lists of Web sites that you have visited or "ear-marked" and wish to return to later. Your browser program will store the paths to those sites and generate a short-cut list for future reference.

HTML (HyperText Mark Up Language) The programming language used to create Web pages so that they can be viewed, read, and accessed from any computer running on any type of operating system.

HTTP (HyperText Transfer Protocol) The communication protocol that allows for Web pages to connect to one another, regardless of what type of operating system is used to display or access the files.

hypertext or hypermedia The system of developing clickable text and objects (pictures, sound, video, etc.) to create links to related documents or different sites on the Internet.

inbox Where incoming e-mail messages are stored and retrieved.

Information Superhighway Nickname for the Internet: a vast highway by which countless pieces of information are made available and exchanged back and forth among its many users.

Internet A world-wide computer network that connects several thousand businesses, schools, research foundations, individuals, and other networks. Anyone with access can log on, communicate via e-mail, and search for various types of information.

Internet address The user ID utilized by an individual or host computer on the Internet. An Internet address is usually associated with the ID used to send and receive e-mail. It consists of the user's ID followed by the domain.

Internet Protocol The method of communication which allows information to be exchanged across the Internet and across varying platforms that may be accessing or sending information.

ISP (Internet Service Providers) Private or public organizations that offer access to the Internet. Most charge a monthly or annual fee and generally offer such features as e-mail accounts, a pre-determined number of hours for Internet access time (or unlimited access for a higher rate), special interest groups, etc.

links Hypertext or hypermedia objects that, once selected, will connect you to related documents or other areas of interest.

login A process by which you gain access to a computer by giving it your username and password. If the computer doesn't recognize your login, access will be denied.

macro virus A virus written in the macro language of a particular program (such as Word) and contained in a program document. When the document is opened, the macro is executed, and the virus usually adds itself to other, similar documents. Macro virus can be only as destructive as the macro language allows.

message header The group of heading fields at the start of every e-mail program, used by the e-mail system to route and otherwise deal with your mail.

meta-tree structured catalog Another term for hierarchically structured catalog.

modem A piece of equipment (either internal or external) that allows a computer to connect to a phone line for the purpose of dialing into the Internet, another network, or an individual computer.

modem speed (baud rate) Indicates at what speed your computer will be able to communicate with a computer on the other end. The higher the rate, the quicker the response time for accessing files and Web pages, processing images, downloading software, etc.

multimedia The process of using various computer formats: pictures, text, sound, movies, etc.

multithread search engines Software that searches the Web sites of other search engines and gathers the results of these searches for your use.

netiquette (Network etiquette) The network equivalent of respectfulness and civility in dealing with people and organizations.

network A group of computers (two or more) that are connected to one another through various means, usually cable or dial-in connections.

Newsgroup A bulletin board of news information. Users specify which news topic they are interested in, and subscribe to receive information on that topic.

newsreader A program that allows you to read and respond to Usenet newsgroups.

offline The process of performing certain tasks, such as preparing e-mail messages, prior to logging onto the Internet.

online The process of performing certain tasks, such as searching the Web or responding to e-mail, while actually logged onto the Internet.

online services Organizations that usually offer Internet access as well as other services, such as shareware, technical support, group discussions, and more. Most online services charge a monthly or annual fee.

operators Words or symbols that modify the search string instead of being part of it.

outbox Where offline e-mail messages are stored. The contents of an outbox are uploaded to the Internet once you log on and prompt your e-mail program to send them.

packet A body of information that is passed through the Internet. It contains the sender's and receiver's addresses and the item that is being sent. Internet Protocol is used to route and process the packet.

platform Refers to the type of computer and its corresponding operating system, such as PC, Macintosh, UNIX. The Internet is a multi-platform entity, meaning that all types of computers can access it.

POP (Post Office Protocol) The method used to transfer e-mail messages from your mail server to your system.

public domain freeware Software that can be used for free; usually the author is anonymous.

quote format A way of displaying text quoted from other e-mail messages, most frequently used in replies. Quoted text usually has a character like ">" at the start of each line. Some e-mail programs let you set the style of quoted material.

search engine A software program that goes out on the Web, seeks Web sites, and catalogs them – usually by downloading their home pages.

search sites Web sites that contain catalogs of Web resources that can be searched by headings, URLs, and key words.

self-extracting archive Macintosh-platform compressed file that does not require external software for decompression. These files usually end with an .sea extension.

self-extracting file PC-platform compressed file that does not require external software for decompression. These files usually end with an .exe extension.

server program A computer program that offers a service to other computer programs called client programs. The FTP server program offers the FTP service to FTP client programs. Server programs usually run in computers you will be connecting to.

server A computer that is accessed by other computers on a network. It usually shares files with or provides other services to the client computers that log onto it.

shareware Computer programs, utilities and other items (fonts, games, etc.) that can be downloaded or distributed free of charge, but with the understanding that if you wish to continue using it, you will send the suggested fee to the developer.

signature A few lines of text automatically appended to the body of an e-mail message. Signatures usually include the sender's address plus other information.

simple search Uses a text string, usually a single word, to search for matches in a search engine's catalog.

.sit file A Macintosh file compressed by using a compression application called StuffIt.

SLIP (Serial Line Internet Protocol) Software that allows for a direct serial connection to the Internet. SLIP allows your computer to become part of the Internet – not just a terminal accessing the Internet. If your computer is set up with SLIP, you can Telnet or FTP other computers directly without having to go through an Internet provider.

SMTP (Simple Mail Transfer Protocol) The method used to transfer e-mail messages between servers and from your system to your mail server.

spiders Another name for search engines.

standalone FTP client program A standalone computer program designed to talk to an FTP server program running at a remote computer site that offers FTP services. The FTP client program can ask for the files you want and send files you wish to deliver. The client program runs in your computer; the server program runs at the site.

start page The opening page within a browser application. This is the page from which all other Web site links are built. A browser's start page is its home page by default, but you can customize your browser to begin with any Web site as your start page.

subject-structured catalog A catalog organized under a few broad subject headings. The number and names of these headings depend on the Web site.

surfing the Internet Exploring various World Wide Web sites and links to search for information on the Internet. Using FTP, WAIS, and Gopher servers can further assist in the surfing/searching process – as can a good Internet browser.

TCP/IP (Transmission Control Protocol/ Internet Protocol) The communication system that is used between networks on the Internet. It checks to make sure that information is being correctly sent and received from one computer to another.

Telnet A program that allows one computer to log on to another host computer. This process allows you to use any of the features available on the host computer, including sharing data and software, participating in interactive discussions, etc.

236

text format file Same as the ASCII format file: a document that has been formatted to be read by almost any computer or program in the world.

text string A string of ASCII characters. The text string may or may not contain operators.

threaded messages Messages grouped so that replies to a message are grouped with the original message. When threaded messages are sorted, threads are kept together.

uploading The process of copying computer files (e-mail, software, documents, etc.) from one's own computer to a remote computer.

URL (Uniform Resource Locator) A locator command used only within the World Wide Web system to create or hunt for linked sites. It operates and looks much like an Internet Address.

Usenet A world-wide discussion system, operating on linked Usenet servers, consisting of a set of newsgroups where articles or messages are posted covering a variety of subjects and interests. You can use your browser or a newsreader program to access the newsgroups available from your Internet provider's Usenet server.

UUencoding One of the encoding schemes, short for UNIX-to-UNIX encoding. UUencoding is common on all platforms, not just UNIX.

virus A small, usually destructive computer program that hides inside innocent-looking programs. Once the virus is executed, it attaches itself to other programs. When triggered, often by the occurrence of a date or time on the computer's internal clock/calendar, it executes a nuisance or damaging function, such as printing a message or reformatting your hard disk.

WAIS (Wide Area Information Servers) A system that allows for searches for information based on actual contents of files, not just file titles.

Web robots Software which automatically searches the Web for new sites.

Web site A location on the Internet that represents a particular company, organization, topic, etc. It normally contains links to more information within a site, as well as suggested links to related sites on the Internet.

World Wide Web (WWW) An easy-to-use system for finding information on the Internet through the use of hypertext or hypermedia linking. Hypertext and hypermedia consist of text and graphic objects that, when you click on them, automatically link you to different areas of a site or to related Internet sites.

zip file PC file compressed with pkzip. Zipped files usually need to be unzipped with pkunzip before they can be used.

Index

1

19thHole.com 131
1travel.com 143

A

AARP 162
Accuracy of Internet information vi
Address bar in Internet Explorer 44
Address Book
    AOL 95
    add entry from mail 98
    create group 98
    delete in AOL 99
    using in AOL 97
    Netscape Messenger 24, 25, 32
    Outlook Express 62
Advocacy
    National Council of Senior
      Citizens 171
    National Council on the Aging 169
    National Senior Citizens
      Law Center 172
    NCPSSM 172
    United Seniors Association 172
Age of Reason.com 168
Airfare
    1travel.com 143
    cheap seats 141
    Continental Airlines - Seniors
      Programs 142
    FareFinder 144
    Hilton Senior HHonors 144
    TWA Senior Travel Pak 141
Aleene's 140
AltaVista 112
America Online (AOL)
    about 77
    add Favorite Places 85
    address book 95
    Browser toolbar 82
    compose mail 91
    delete address book entry 99

    delete Favorite Places 86
    download attachment 102
    exit 80
    Favorite places 85
    font size 80
    forward mail 94
    GO TO AOL NETFIND 82
    GO TO THE WEB 82
    Help 80
    history list 87
    Home 83
    home page 78
    Internet button 81
    Location line 83
    mail help 94
    menu 78
    open a Web site 82
    print Web pages 89
    read new mail 90
    Reload 83, 84
    reply to mail 93
    save Web pages 88
    send a message 93
    start 77
    status bar 84
    stop a load or search 84
    Stop 84
    toolbar 78
    using address book entry 97
    view Favorite Places 86
ANSWERS Magazine 197
Arts and crafts 137
    Aleene's 140
    I-Craft 138
    Knitting 140
    Michaels: The Arts and
      Crafts Store 137
    Mining Co. Crafts for Kids 140
    www.quiltersweb.com 140
Ask Dr. Weil 183
Assumptions of this book iv
Attachments
    AOL 100, 102

Netscape Messenger................. 33, 36
Outlook Express 75
view in Netscape Messenger........... 33
AutoSearch, Internet Explorer 49

B

Baker Boulanger................................. 122
Before I Die Home Page.................... 219
Bereavement and
    Hospice Support Netline................ 219
Better Homes and Gardens
    Kitchen....................................... 123
    Gardening Home Page.................. 127
Betty Crocker..................................... 123
Binary files 33
Bingo 136
Burpee Web site 130

C

Channels, AOL 79
Cheap seats, (See Airfare)
CNN Interactive 194
Colorado Life 198
Compose a message
    Netscape Messenger....................... 23
    Outlook Express 62
    AOL 91
Conquest 199
Continental Airlines -
    Seniors Programs.......................... 142
Cooking 118–23
    Baker Boulanger............................ 122
    Better Homes and
        Gardens Kitchen........................ 123
    Betty Crocker................................ 123
    Epicurious..................................... 118
    Food Network's CyberKitchen....... 120
    Internet Chef On-Line
        Magazine................................. 123
Crafts 137
Crawlers 106
Cryptogram... 135
CryptoPlus 135
CyberKitchen, Food Network............. 120

D

Default save location in AOL 104
Deja News 202

Delta Society...................................... 161
Dental ResourceNet 184
Digitalchef 126
Directories (search) 106
Douglas Gerlach's
    Invest-O-Rama 191
Download attachment, AOL.............. 102

E

Elderhostel... 145
ElderTreks 146
Epicurious 118
Errors 216
Exit
    AOL 80
    Internet Explorer 42
    Netscape... 6
Extended Care Information Network.. 178

F

Family trees, See Genealogy
Fancy Foods Gourmet Club.............. 125
FareFinder 144
Favorites
    add in AOL..................................... 85
    create new in Internet Explorer........ 49
    delete in AOL 86
    Internet Explorer 44, 47
    Internet Explorer 46
    open Web site in
        Internet Explorer 47
    view in AOL................................... 86
Finances 187–91
    Douglas Gerlach's
        Invest-O-Rama 191
    Morningstar................................... 189
    Motley Fool Finance and Folly....... 191
    The Street..................................... 190
    Yahoo! Finance............................. 187
Font size
    AOL 80
    Internet Explorer 39
    Netscape... 17
Food Network 120
Forward mail
    AOL 83, 94
    Internet Explorer 43
    Netscape Messenger................. 18, 29

Outlook Express 67
Foundation For Grandparenting 155
Foundation for Osteoporosis
    Research and Education 181
Fun and games................................. 131
    19thHole.com 131
    CryptoPlus................................. 135
    Gamesville................................. 136
    Jeopardy Online 136
    Yahoo! Games........................... 133
Funsites Guide to Web sites
    for Seniors & Retirement 168

G

Games 131-36
Gamesville 136
Garden Solutions 130
Gardening..................................... 127–30
    Better Homes and Gardens:
        Gardening Home Page.............. 127
    Burpee Web Site 130
    Garden Solutions 130
    GardenNet................................. 128
    Gardenscape Ltd.: Fine Garden
        Tools & Accessories 130
    Rose Resource............................ 129
GardenNet.................................... 128
Gardenscape Ltd.: Fine Garden
    Tools & Accessories 130
Genealogy 150
    Genealogy Gateway 153
    Genealogy Home Page 154
    Genealogy Links & Information 154
    Genealogy—AT&T WorldNet
        Service................................. 150
    Helm's Genealogy Toolbox 151
    Mining Co. 151
    RootsWeb.................................. 154
    USGenWeb Project 152
Golden Escapes: Tours
    for the 50 plus Traveler................. 148
Golf 132
Gourmet Goodies 124
    Digitalchef................................. 126
    Fancy Foods Gourmet Club 125
    Virtual Vineyards 124
    Wine Navigator 126
Grand Circle Travel Online 149
Grand Times Magazine 197

Grandparenting........................... 155–57
    Foundation For Grandparenting 155
    Grandparenting—Senior Living 156
    Grandtravel 157
Grandparenting—Senior Living 156
Grandtravel 157

H

Healthfinder 179
Healthy Paws................................ 161
Healthy Pets 160
Helm's Genealogy Toolbox.............. 151
Help
    AOL... 80
    search site 111
Help with computers
    Help-Site.com 214
    Internet Help Desk 214
    SeniorNet.................................. 213
    Seniors Helping Seniors 212
Help-Site.com 214
Hilton Senior HHonors 144
History
    Channels Explorer 44
    Internet Explorer 44
History list
    AOL... 87
Home
    Extended Care
        Information Network................. 178
    HUD: Senior Citizens 173
    LivOn Senior Living
        Online Network...................... 177
    Retirement Net.......................... 175
    Senior Living Alternatives 176
    Senior Living Home Page 178
Home page
    AOL...................................... 78, 83
    Internet Explorer 40, 43
Homecare Industry 220
Hospice Hands 220
HUD: Senior Citizens....................... 173
Hypertension Network 185

I

ICE... 115
I-Craft... 138

If You're Over 65 and
  Feeling Depressed 219
International Herald Tribune 195
Internet
  cautions vi
  requirements iv
Internet Chef On-Line Magazine 123
Internet Connection Wizard
  Outlook Express 51
Internet Explorer
  about 39
  Address bar 44
  AutoSearch 49
  create new Favorites folder 49
  exit 42
  Favorites folder 46
  font size change 39
  open Web site 44
  start 38
Internet Help Desk 214
Internet Mailing Lists
  Guides and Resources 211

J

Jeopardy Online 136

K

Keyword
  newsgroups 204
  AOL 79
Kids' Club Projects 138
Knitting 140

L

Legislation, See Advocacy
Links to Hospice Sites 220
Liszt 208
LivOn Senior Living Online Network .. 177

M

Magazines
  ANSWERS Magazine 197
  Colorado Life 198
  Conquest 199
  Grand Times Magazine 197
  Maryland Maturity Lifestyles 199
  New Choices 200

Senior Beacon 198
Senior Connection 200
Senior Magazine 198
Senior News Network
  by SeniorCom 196
SNN Global Edition 200
Southern California Senior Life 199
Mail
  AOL 79
  help in AOL 94
  Internet Explorer 44
  Netscape Messenger 16
  Outlook Express 54, 56, 57, 58
Mailing Lists 207–11
  helpful hints 211
  Internet Mailing Lists
    Guides and Resources 211
  Liszt 208
  Publicly Accessible
    Mailing Lists 211
  Tile.net-Lists 211
  Yahoo! Mailing Lists 210
Maryland Maturity Lifestyles 199
Mayo Health Oasis 185
MedAccess 186
Medical advice
  Ask Dr. Weil 183
  Dental ResourceNet 184
  Foundation for Osteoporosis
    Research and Education 181
  Healthfinder 179
  Hypertension Network 185
  Mayo Health Oasis 185
  MedAccess 186
  Menopause Online 182
  National Institute of Mental
    Health's Anxiety Disorders 186
  OncoLink 185
  Osteoporosis Center 186
  Yahoo! Health Topic 186
Menopause Online 182
Message
  close in Netscape Messenger 21
  compose in Outlook Express 62
  forward in AOL 94
  forward in Netscape Messenger 29
  read in AOL 90
  read in Netscape Messenger 20
  read in Outlook Express 58
  reply in AOL 93

242

reply in Netscape Messenger 27
reply in Outlook Express 66
retrieve in Outlook Express 55
send in AOL 93
send in Netscape Messenger 24
send in Outlook Express 63
Michaels: The Arts and Crafts
  Store 137
Microsoft Internet Explorer,
  See Internet Explorer
Mining Co.
  grandparenting 157
  Crafts for Kids 140
Money, See Finances
Morningstar 189
Motley Fool Finance and Folly 191
MSNBC 195

N

National Council of
  Senior Citizens 171
National Council on the Aging 169
National Hospice Organization 220
National Institute of Mental
  Health's Anxiety Disorders 186
National Senior Citizens
  Law Center 172
Native American
  genealogy 154
NCOA, See National Council
  on the Aging 170
NCPSSM 172
Netscape
  font size 17
  Personal address book 30
  Stop button 83
Netscape Collabra 204
Netscape Messenger
  close a message 21
  compose a message 23
  configure 15
  delete a message 22
  exit 6
  file attachments 33
  forward a message 29
  identity settings 15
  Mail Server 16
  message composition 24
  Message List window 17

Next button 21
print a message 22
Quote button 29
read a message 20
save attached file 35
save password 20
send a message 24
start 14
toolbar 18
view attachments 33
New Choices 200
New York Times on the Web 192
News
  CNN Interactive 194
  International Herald Tribune 195
  MSNBC 195
  New York Times on the Web 192
  NewsWorks 195
Newsgroups
  accessing through ISP 204
  categories 205
  defined 201
  Deja News 202
  helpful hints 206
NewsWorks 195

O

OncoLink 185
Osteoporosis Center 186
Outlook Express 204
  attach a file 75
  Column headings 58
  compose a message 62
  configure 50
  Internet Connection Wizard 51
  Mail Folder list 54, 57
  Mail toolbar 58
  Mail window 56
  Message List pane 57
  Next button 60
  Outbox folder 64
  Personal Address Book 68
  read a message 58
  read mail shortcut 56
  reply to a message 66
  retrieve new messages 55
  save an attached file 74
  send a message 63

send a message from
   Outbox folder 65
shortcuts 54
start.. 50
store a message in
   Outbox folder 65
view attached files 71

P

Paperclip icon
   Netscape Messenger...................... 33
   Outlook Express 71
Password
   save in Netscape Messenger 20
Personal address book
   Netscape 30
   Outlook Express 68
Pet care
   Delta Society 161
   Healthy Paws................................ 161
   Healthy Pets 160
   Pet Channel................................... 158
   Purina Pets for
      People Program..................... 161
   Senior Citizens Best Friends:
      Pets 161
Pet Channel.................................... 158
Pet horoscopes............................... 159
Print
   AOL 89
   Netscape Messenger................. 19, 22
   Outlook Express 61
Projects
   I-Craft... 139
   Michaels 138
Publicly Accessible Mailing Lists 211
Purina Pets for People Program........ 161

Q

QTW-Senior Travel........................... 149
Quilters 140

R

Read a message
   AOL 90
   Netscape Messenger...................... 20
   Outlook Express 56, 58
Recipes

Baker Boulanger 122
Epicurious....................................... 119
Food Network 121
Refine a search............................... 109
Reply to a message
   AOL... 93
   Netscape Messenger...................... 27
   Outlook Express 66
Retirement Net................................. 175
RootsWeb 154
Rose Resource 129

S

Save attached file
   Netscape Messenger...................... 35
   Outlook Express 74
Save Web pages in AOL
Search
   AltaVista....................................... 112
   basics... 107
   directories 106
   engines 105
   Help 111
   multi-threaded.............................. 106
   refine a search 109
   results 108
   results 109
   simple 108
   text string 107
   Yahoo! 114
Security...vi
Security
   Netscape Messenger................. 19, 24
Send a message
   AOL.. 93, 94
   Netscape Messenger........... 24, 27, 29
   Outlook Express 63, 68
Senior Beacon 198
Senior Citizens Best Friends:
   Pets... 161
Senior Connection 200
Senior Cyborgs................................ 167
Senior Living Alternatives 176
Senior Living Home Page 178
Senior Magazine.............................. 198
Senior News Network by
   SeniorCom.................................... 196
SeniorCom....................................... 164
SeniorNet.. 213

Index

Seniors Helping Seniors 212
Seniors resources 162–68
  AARP 162
  Age of Reason.com 168
  Funsites Guide to Web sites for
    Seniors & Retirement 168
  Senior Cyborgs 167
  SeniorCom 164
  Seniors-Site.com 168
  ThirdAge 166
Seniors-Site.com 168
SNN Global Edition 200
Southern California Senior Life 199
Spelling
  Netscape Messenger 24, 27
Spiders 106
Start
  AOL 77
  Internet Explorer 38
  Netscape Messenger 14
  Outlook Express 50
Status bar
  AOL 84
Stop a load or search
  AOL 84
  Internet Explorer 43
  Netscape 83
  Netscape Messenger 24
Support Resource
  Before I Die Home Page 219
  Bereavement and Hospice
    Support Netline 219
  Homecare Industry 220
  Hospice Hands 220
  If You're Over 65 and
    Feeling Depressed 219
  Links to Hospice Sites 220
  National Hospice Organization 220
  WidowNet 220

T

Text string 107
The Street 190
ThirdAge 166
ThirdAge Marketplace -
  The Cruise Center 149

Tile.net-Lists 211
Travel (See also Airfare) 145
  cheap seats 141
  Elderhostel 145
  ElderTreks 146
  Golden Escapes: Tours for
    the 50 plus Traveler 148
  Grand Circle Travel Online 149
  Grandtravel 157
  QTW-Senior Travel 149
  ThirdAge Marketplace -
    The Cruise Center 149
Troubleshooting URLs 215–18
TWA Senior Travel Pak 141

U

United Seniors Association 172
URL defined 215
URL troubleshooting 215–18
Usenet
  Americal Online 204
  Netscape Collabra 204
  Outlook Express 204

V

Virtual Vineyards 124
Viruses vi

W

Web searches 112
WidowNet 220
Wine 124, 126
Wine Navigator 126
www.quiltersweb.com 140

Y

Yahoo! 112, 114
Yahoo! Finance 187
Yahoo! Games 133
Yahoo! Health Topic 186
Yahoo! Mailing Lists 210
You Have Mail (AOL) 90

NEW at ddcpub.com!

Visit the DDC Web Rover Gallery
Go to **www.ddcpub.com**
and click on the *Web Rover Gallery* link

The **DDC Web Rover** hunts the Internet every week, sniffing out the best sites on the Web.

In the **DDC Web Rover Gallery**, you'll find links to great Web Rov recommended resources for students, bargain hunters, sales people, managers, seniors. You'll also find great entertainment, leisure, and vacation sites.

If you are on the scent of a Web site you find interesting, DDC would like to hear from you. Click on the Web Rover's link and submit the site and the reason you like it. If we list it in the Galle you'll receive a free Computer and Internet dictionary.*

We search the Web so you don't have to!

*This is a limited time offer.